Brainarium
Exercise Your
Creativity

Stuart Pink

DEDICATION

To my two favorite creative geniuses:

Jonathan

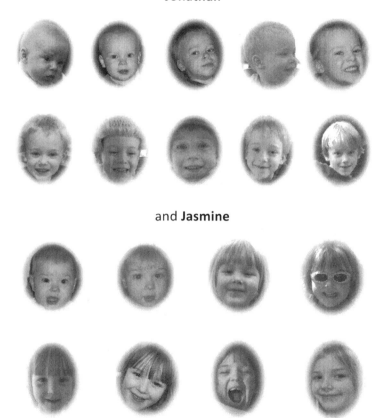

and **Jasmine**

And in loving memory of my mother, Judy Pink.

CONTENTS

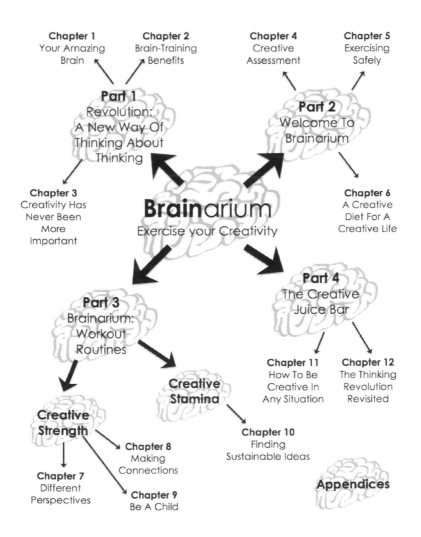

Chapter 1
Your Amazing Brain

Chapter 2
Brain-Training Benefits

Chapter 4
Creative Assessment

Chapter 5
Exercising Safely

Part 1
Revolution: A New Way Of Thinking About Thinking

Part 2
Welcome To Brainarium

Chapter 3
Creativity Has Never Been More Important

Brainarium
Exercise your Creativity

Chapter 6
A Creative Diet For A Creative Life

Part 3
Brainarium: Workout Routines

Part 4
The Creative Juice Bar

Chapter 11
How To Be Creative In Any Situation

Chapter 12
The Thinking Revolution Revisited

Creative Stamina

Creative Strength

Chapter 10
Finding Sustainable Ideas

Chapter 8
Making Connections

Chapter 7
Different Perspectives

Chapter 9
Be A Child

Appendices

ACKNOWLEDGMENTS

Writing a book about creativity entails an unusual risk. It does not feel acceptable to claim a lack of inspiration at any point because surely the creative solution lies within the pages of the book itself! As with all creative projects, encouragement and support are hugely important. I am incredibly grateful to my family and friends for all their patience, love, support and assistance that have enabled me to complete this book.

Thank you, Ray Pink, Zara Hardy and Phill Hardy for being there for me through thick and thin.
Thank you, Kat Zonghetti for being the best girlfriend ever and for changing my life.
Thank you, Matt Zonghetti for some very helpful suggestions.

As I have laboured in finalising this book I have endeavoured to suppress any unfavourable, personalised tendencies towards using misspelt British English rather than the localised American version practised where I live. Please humour me if any mistakes have materialised as a result of my inability to edit skilfully.

Declaration of Creativity

We hold these truths to be self-evident:

1. "Creativity" is not an elitist word.
2. Everyone is creative.
3. Creativity is essential to a healthy, happy, purposeful life.
4. Creativity is essential for future human success.
5. Creativity can be learned and should be exercised.
6. Creativity should be encouraged and appreciated whenever possible.

_____   _____

Signed   Date

Part 1

Revolution: A New Way Of Thinking About Thinking

You just read the Declaration of Creativity. Did you sign it? If not, the job of this book is to convince you that creativity is essential and that it is part of who you are. Too many people fail to recognize that or don't even realize how creative they are.

Imagine two worlds, identical in every way except for one thing. The first world is like ours. Let's call it Planet Earth. The other is a world without any creativity. Because it lacks creativity, let's call it Planet Dearth.

What would human life be like on Planet Dearth? There would be no cars, no computers, and no entertainment. Without creativity, there would be no imagination, so you couldn't even do this exercise! In fact, even our most basic needs – drinking, eating, sleeping, and clothing – have involved creativity to make them more interesting or effective. **About the only thing you do which requires no creativity is breathing!**

Yet if you were to ask most people, they would probably say that they are not creative! Even though they have been learning and creating since birth, they have allowed themselves to think that creativity does not belong to them, but rather only a select few. This is crazy! Imagine if we treated our ability to speak a language the same way:

"I used to be okay at speaking English, but I'm not very good at it now. I'm scared to do it. I'll leave speaking English to the experts like actors and politicians!"

Doesn't that sound utterly ridiculous? There is no more a monopoly on being creative than there is on speaking a language. Creativity is something we all do and the sooner we all recognize this the better. (We can undoubtedly learn how to improve our creativity and that is what this book is about!)

Creativity is not only *the* essential skill in our 21st century world, but it also plays a key part in our health and overall wellbeing. It's high time we learned more about it and started taking it seriously.

Part 1 of this book will explain why creativity is more important than ever before and how humans possess a unique gift to be creative. It will also show that creativity can be learned and should be exercised.

Part 2 will introduce Brainarium. You can think of it as a gymnasium for the brain where you can work up a mental sweat by doing creative exercises. You can assess your creative aptitude here as well as learning some important safety tips before working out.

Part 3 explains the two stages of the creative process and simplifies all creativity down to its overriding themes. First, there are Creative Strength exercises. These are useful for generating lots of different ideas. Then the Creative Stamina exercises can be used for evaluating and choosing the best ideas from those previously generated.

Finally, Part 4 brings everything together. The exercises in this book will give you a simple framework to be creative in any situation. Creativity doesn't need to be lonely though. Let's fight the Thinking Revolution together!

Chapter 1

Your Amazing Brain

Your life starts with two amazing and miraculous facts: 1) the miracle of **your existence** and 2) the miracle of **your brain**.

1) The miracle of your existence

The odds of you being born were essentially zero. Thousands of generations of your ancestors had to find each other and reproduce. Your exact ancestral sperm and eggs had to meet on every occasion. The odds of you existing have been calculated as 1 in $10^{2,685,000}$.[1] Trying to understand this number is almost impossible but let's try by imagining you were playing a game of roulette to decide if you would be born. Instead of using a normal roulette wheel, you have to use one with as many numbers as there are atoms in the universe.[2] You are one of those numbers and the ball must land on your number for you to be born. Against the most spectacular odds ever, the ball lands on your number! This is unbelievable! But we're not done. To be born, you then have to do exactly the same thing again 33,500 times in a row!

It could never happen ... except that in the case of your birth, it did happen! Your birth was the most unlikely lottery win ever. You are quite literally a miracle. Do you feel special now?

2) The miracle of your brain

But that's not all. You were born with an organ that many scientists consider to be the most complex structure in the known universe: a human brain. Much is often made of the inequality that many of earth's seven billion inhabitants are born into, but the possession of a human brain is both a great leveler and a priceless gift. To understand just how precious it is, let's consider a few facts about it.

How is the brain wired?

The brain is made up of nerve cells called **neurons**. A neuron processes and transmits information through electrical and chemical signals. Your brain has 100 billion neurons in it. That is about the same as the number of stars in our galaxy!

The neurons are connected by **synapses**. If a neuron is the telephone, a synapse is the connection between phones. An infant has one quadrillion (or 1,000,000,000,000,000) synapses. That is about the same number as all of the ants on earth!

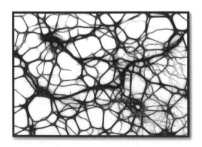

An infant actually has roughly twice as many con-nections as an adult does because, from the age of 11, the brain starts pruning the connections. Connections that are used repeatedly become permanent; those that are not are eliminated. It is very much a case of **"use it or lose it**!" There is a good reason for this pruning. It helps to keep the brain efficient and uncluttered.

Compare the experience of driving a car to when you first learned. There is much that you do automatically without much effort now because it has become an efficient, routine experience. This frees your brain up to focus on other things.

Cool brain facts

- Your brain is actually three brains that have evolved over time:

  - The oldest is the **reptilian brain** that processes **instincts.**

  - Next, there is the **limbic system** that processes **emotions.**

  - Finally, the biggest part is the **neo-cortex** that processes **higher-order thinking.**

- Your brain weighs about 3 lbs.

- Your brain uses 20% of the blood circulating in your body and 20% of the oxygen you breathe.

- The brain can feel no pain – it has no pain receptors.

- The brain can send information at 250mph – faster than a racing car!

- **Your** brain uses about 15-20 watts to power itself – the same as a dim light bulb!

Right brain, left brain, whole brain

The brain has two hemispheres and much has been made of the supposed specializations of different functions on each side. There is some truth to these:

Left Brain		Right Brain
• Speech and Language • Logic • Number • Analysis • Detail-oriented • Controls right side of body		• Pattern recognition • Spatial skills • Rhythm and music • Images and pictures • Focused on big picture • Daydreaming • Controls left side of body

But there is not much sense in claiming to be either right-brained or left-brained. The hemispheres are connected by the corpus callosum, a bundle of nerve tissue that passes information between them. Everyone uses and relies on both sides of the brain all the time. Creativity is not the sole domain of the right brain. Both sides have functions that enable creativity and so **the only sensible approach to creativity (and to life) is a whole-brained one**.

Neuroplasticity and exercise

Now comes the exciting bit. Conventional wisdom used to be that once you reached adulthood, your brain stopped growing and was fixed in the way it had developed up to that point. That is now known to be wrong. Throughout your life, your brain continues to make new neurons in response to mental activity. Every time you have a new thought or recall a memory, a new brain connection is made between two or more brain cells. This means that, **if you use it, your brain continues to develop throughout your life.** This is called **neuroplasticity** or **brain plasticity.**

Neuroplasticity is such a miracle that even people born with only half a brain have been able to live relatively normal lives because of the brain's ability to rewire itself. Michelle Mack, a woman from Virginia, has no left hemisphere but her right hemisphere took over her speech and language functions.[3] A 10-year old girl in Germany has no right hemisphere but developed both fields of vision in one eye because her brain rewired itself.[4]

Though these examples occurred out of necessity, you can choose to use neuroplasticity to your advantage. Michael Merzenich, a leading researcher on brain plasticity, claims that we can change the structure of the brain to allow it to function more healthily and to increase its capacity to learn.[5]

The ability to create new paths in the brain does not mean that it is easy. If you have ever driven on a highway in a snowstorm, you will know that it is much easier (and safer) to follow the established path of the car in front. A new path in the snow will be slippery at first but as it is used more often and becomes established it is easier to navigate. Plasticity is reminiscent of this and therefore has what psychiatrist Norman Doidge calls a paradox.[6] On the one hand, it can enable us to change our brains and our behavior, but on the other hand, it can also cause us to become more rigid and set in our ways if we stick to following the same path.

The important point to note however is that **we actually have a choice about how healthy we want our brains to be.**

How much is the brain worth?

Is it possible to put a value on this remarkable piece of equipment in you? In one sense, of course, it is priceless. Your brain is not something to give up willingly to someone else because you can't live without it! Nor if you were the richest person on earth would you have enough money to be able to create an actual brain.

In 2013, President Obama announced the creation of the White House BRAIN Initiative (Brain Research through Advancing Innovative Neurotechnologies) with the goal of revolutionizing our understanding of the brain. This was considered so important that initial funding was $100 million with over $300 million being raised since.[7]

But perhaps a better way to value the brain is to compare it to a supercomputer. No one knows exactly how many calculations a human brain can perform each second. One estimate is one quadrillion.[8] In supercomputer terms that is known as one petaflop. The world's first petaflop computer, the IBM Roadrunner, was built in 2008 for $100 million. But the human brain is much more efficient than such a machine. Remember, it uses just 20 watts of power! It's been estimated that to replicate the computing power of the human brain would require a computer that runs at 38 petaflops.[9] As of 2016, only one supercomputer in the world is more powerful than this - the Sunway TaihuLight supercomputer in China, which runs at nearly 93 petaflops[10] and cost $270 million.[11]

Whichever way you look at it, **it seems reasonable to say that you have at least a $100 million piece of equipment sitting in your head!** And unlike a computer, your brain can change itself and keep getting better...

Stop and think about this. You might buy new running shoes and leave them in their box. But if someone dropped a $100 million computer off at your house, you'd rush to get it out of its box, wouldn't you? You certainly wouldn't leave it there unused. The same goes with your brain. Don't leave it in its box!

But unwrapping your $100 million supercomputer is not enough. Now you need to work out what to do with it. Should you use it for simple calculations or should you try to do something amazing with it? That is the choice you must make every day with your brain.

And one of the most amazing things you can do with your brain is BE CREATIVE!

Your Amazing Brain – Summary

- The chances of you existing were practically zero yet here you are reading this!

- Your brain has one billion **neurons** (nerve cells) and one quadrillion **synapses** (connections).

- Your brain has two hemispheres, which specialize in certain functions, but both are equally important.

- Your brain continues to change throughout your life. This is called **neuroplasticity**.

- Your brain might be worth $100 million. You should use it and exercise it!

Chapter 2

Brain-Training Benefits

Why train the brain?

55 million Americans belong to a gym and over five billion gym visits were made in 2014.[12] Many more people exercise at home, outdoors or playing sports. Yet for some reason, we have never placed mental fitness on the same pedestal as physical fitness. There is, however, evidence that interest in brain-training is growing. A recent survey showed that three-quarters of adults aged 40+ are concerned about their brain health declining in the future and that nearly all adults (98%) feel it is important to maintain or improve brain health.[13] As Michael Merzenich puts it, **"We've got to do something about the mental lifespan, to extend it out and into the body's lifespan."**[14] In this chapter, we will look first at how exercising the brain works and then consider a number of specific benefits to exercising creativity.

1) How exercising the brain works

We have seen that the brain's plasticity allows it to continue developing throughout our lives but how does it actually work?

The brain is a muscle that grows with exercise. Post-mortem examinations have shown that education increases the number of branches among neurons and this, in turn, drives the neurons further apart increasing the size of the brain.[15] When you perform a task, the neurons in your brain associated with the component parts of that task will "fire" or send an electrical signal. When two neurons fire together at the same time, chemical changes occur in both causing them to connect together more strongly. Neuroscientist Carla Shatz describes it as, **"neurons that fire together wire together."**[16] When neurons connect together more strongly we become better at the particular task we are doing and ultimately this can lead to mastery of the task. This is as true for creativity as for anything else. As brain researcher Charles Limb, puts it, **"artists become creative experts by practicing how to be creative."**[17]

Babies and young children start with a natural advantage here. Everything is new to them and their brains are so plastic that just exposing them to new stimuli can change their structure. This is because their brains' ability to learn is always on at the start of life.[18] As we grow older we need to work harder to keep our brain learning and in particular work on new skills rather than just reusing the skills that we already have. **Because creativity inherently involves something new, it is ideal for the purpose of training your brain.**

A war of nerves

Plasticity is competitive. We have already mentioned the importance of "use it or lose it" when it comes to your brain. Each part of the brain is allocated to different skills. If those skills stop being used then that space is turned over to other skills that are used, much like freeing up storage space on a computer.[19] This explains why blind people can find their other senses heightened. The part of their brains that would have been used for sight is available for other uses.

In some ways this is reminiscent of the way sea coral fights a turf war with its closest neighbors, trying to take over and fill the space available. As you sit here reading this, there is literally a war of nerves occurring in your brain!

A question of mind over matter

One of the most well-known techniques that successful, high achieving people use their brains for is visualization. But just how powerful is the mind? Alvaro Pascual-Leone, Professor of Neurology at Harvard, conducted an experiment where he taught two groups of people how to play the piano. One group actually played music while the other group just sat in front of a keyboard and imagined playing. Both groups learned to play and both groups showed similar changes to the maps of their brains! The group that actually practiced did outperform the "imaginary practice" group, but mental practice definitely helped the second group learn a physical skill.[20]

This close link between imagining and actually performing an action is a result of the fact that the brain reacts in a very similar way in both situations. This could be taken to its ultimate extreme – can you just imagine physical exercise instead of actually doing it? In another experiment by Erin Shackell and Lionel Standing, a group of people practiced daily hip flexions (an exercise raising a leg) while a second group just imagined the exercise. After two weeks, both groups experienced substantial (and similar) increases in strength.[21] Clearly, your brain has great power!

17

Creative or logical brain-training?

At this point, I need to make an important distinction. When you typically hear about brain-training, brain games or mental puzzles, the context is almost always one that refers to logical puzzles or exercises. By logical, I mean something that has an objectively correct answer. Chess problems, Sudoku puzzles, crosswords and even games like Pictionary (where you draw a picture that has to be recognized by your teammates) all require a logical, correct answer. The good news about creative exercise is that there is no correct answer! Anything can be valid. The bad news about creative exercise is that there is no correct answer! Some people are uncomfortable when they leave the world of black and white, right and wrong. I am a huge fan of logical games and puzzles and I think they are fantastic for exercising the brain. This book, however, is about the missing piece – the importance of creative exercise.

2) Benefits of exercising creativity

I believe that the benefits of exercising creativity can be split into four broad categories. Although an individual's interest in creativity may arise through any one of the four categories, all four are of great importance to every human being. The four categories, which we will consider in turn, are:

- **Health benefits**
- **Happiness and wellbeing**
- **Purpose and fulfillment**
- **Creative benefits**

I would think that most people would automatically wish for a life that is healthy, happy, purposeful and fulfilling (i.e. the first three categories). Once the nature of the changing world in which we live is understood (see Chapter 3), the creative benefits must surely be desired too.

A) Health benefits

There are many benefits to leading a creative life that have nothing to do with health. However, if there were health benefits to practicing creativity then that would certainly be a major reason to be more creative.

Recent years have seen many organizations offer brain-training games.[22] These are typically computer games that test cognitive skills such as memory, attention and reaction speed. A large group of neuroscientists considers that many of the claims made relating to the health benefits of these brain-training games are exaggerated or misleading. In particular, when a person improves their performance on a particular brain game, it is not clear whether they are just improving their skills at that game or whether there is any wider benefit. They concluded that "when researchers follow people across their adult lives, they find that those who live cognitively active, socially connected lives and maintain healthy lifestyles are less likely to suffer debilitating illness and early cognitive decline in their golden years than their sedentary, cognitively and socially disengaged counterparts."[23] This does, however, point to how creative exercise can be beneficial. Creativity is a cognitively active skill, which means that practicing and applying it can definitely benefit you.

An area of particular interest with regard to brain-training is whether it can delay or even help cure Alzheimer's disease. Alzheimer's is a serious disease that attacks the neurons in the brain and is the most common form of dementia. Symptoms include memory loss and problems with thinking and behavior. In America, over five million adults have Alzheimer's and one in three seniors will die as a result of Alzheimer's or another form of dementia. These figures are set to increase as population and life expectancy increase. By 2050, it's estimated that the cost of caring for Alzheimer's patients in America will be $1 trillion.[24] To date, there has not been proof that brain-training can cure or delay Alzheimer's but given the prevalence and serious impact of Alzheimer's, there will no doubt continue to be much research done. Even without conclusive proof of the benefits of brain-training, one could argue that if dementia attacks neurons in the brain then exercising those neurons must be a good idea.

However, recent research by Professor David A. Bennett has shown something very interesting. Most brains in old age actually show signs of Alzheimer's disease. Despite this, some elderly people seem not to suffer any symptoms. The key difference for those people that suffer no symptoms is that they appear to have a greater cognitive reserve to fall back upon. In other words (and very simplistically), people with bigger brains can afford to lose more of them to the degenerative attack of dementia before they suffer the effects of dementia. The million-dollar question (for the $100 million brain) is what builds cognitive reserve? The early answers appear to be a mixture of factors within and without your control. Two big factors are your genes and your education. Further beneficial factors (that happen also to be relevant to the discussion in this book) include engaging in regular cognitive activity, strengthening social ties, exploring new things, being happy, and engaging in meaningful activities.[25] It would therefore appear that many aspects of a creative life are beneficial to building a better brain.

While research into the effects of brain-training continues, there is no doubt that creativity and creative therapies are also increasingly being used to help people with dementia, at least in a palliative care sense. *MeetMe* is a successful program run by the Museum of Modern Art in New York to make art accessible for people with dementia, by showing groups around the museum and discussing certain paintings with them.[26] Benefits observed include improving the quality of life of the participants and allowing them to be self-expressive in ways that were not possible before.[27] Interestingly, the experience was found to be positive and stress relieving for the caregivers who accompanied the participants too.

The National Coalition of Creative Arts Therapies Associations represents various organizations that use the creative arts for therapy (for example art, dance, music, poetry). A few examples they list of the numerous health benefits from participating in such creative arts therapies are:

- **Mental Health Needs** - making nonthreatening experiences for the exploration of feelings and therapeutic issues, such as self-esteem or personal insight.

- **Chronic Illness** - distracting people from pain and helping relaxation.

- **Head Injuries** - using group experiences to encourage self-expression, communication, and socialization, and to facilitate cognitive retraining.

- **Physical Disabilities** - using arts experiences to promote rehabilitative goals and to increase motivation.

- **Developmental Disabilities** - teaching cognitive, motor, and daily living skills through the arts.[28]

In the future, as we start to learn more about the brain and the illnesses that affect it, we will no doubt be in a better position to look after our mental health. In the meantime though, surely it makes sense to use creativity to keep the brain active and healthy?

B) Happiness and wellbeing

Do you ever wish you could escape from the pressures and stresses of your life? I remember when I used to work as an attorney in London and New York, that work became all-consuming. Emails were constantly received around the clock and even when away from the office, it became impossible to avoid thinking about work. It reached the point that if I took a week off work, I could only relax on the Wednesday in the middle of the week. It took me four days to wind down from work after which point I then spent the last four days anticipating my return to work!

One November weekend, I visited the Lost Gardens of Heligan in Cornwall, England. There was an art festival on and visitors were invited to sit down and draw a plate of autumnal vegetables. I spent half an hour sketching my *"Still Life of a Pumpkin."* Afterward, I realized that for the whole time I had been totally absorbed in the process and completely lost myself.

I forgot all about work and the other things that were bothering me. This is the state of mind that Mihaly Csikszentmihalyi describes as **"flow"** or being in the zone.[29] **Creativity is enjoyable and can relieve stress for anyone, regardless of how healthy they otherwise are.**

C) Purpose and fulfillment

Creativity is a fundamental purpose of being human. It is what we were born to do and what makes us different from other animals. Author and high performance coach Brendon Burchard says, **"creative expression is our ultimate demonstration of who we are in life."** In proof of this, we've been expressing our creativity since the dawn of time. The oldest art is thought to be half a million years old. Our distant ancestors were carving with sharks' teeth on mollusk shells. Then, 40,000 years ago came cave paintings. Imagine that. When the first cave painting was made, it was modern art! Even now, one of the earliest pleasures any toddler can have is making marks on paper, chalkboards or, if you are unlucky, your furniture. As we get older, this turns into doodling. Evidently, there is something inherently satisfying and fulfilling about making a mark.

In the 1960s, psychologist Abraham Maslow identified a pyramid-shaped hierarchy of needs in human life. The basic needs are those essential to sustaining life and safety. Then come love and belonging. At the top of his pyramid is self-actualization which can be defined as the fulfillment of one's talent and potential. This is closely related to one's purpose in life and we can therefore say that creativity is very much part of self-actualization.

Having purpose in life is so important and increasingly so for today's millennial generation. It could be argued that the search for purpose and meaning is one of their defining traits and one reason why they quickly move jobs if they are not satisfied. Viktor Frankl discussed the role of purpose and hope in one of history's darkest hours. In his book, *Man's Search for Meaning*, where he describes surviving three years in Nazi concentration camps, he observed the increased death rate among camp inmates between Christmas 1944 and New Year's Day 1945.

There was no obvious external reason for this and he concluded that the cause was simply that the inmates had given up after their hopes of returning home for Christmas had passed.[30]

In writing about the solution to depression, authors Kalle Lasn and Bruce Grierson consider that **"The most promising way to happiness is, perhaps, through creativity, through literally creating a fulfilling life for yourself by identifying some unique talent or passion and devoting a good part of your energy to it, forever."**[31]

When the time comes to leave your legacy there are only two physical things you can leave behind: your children and your creations. When you're gone, they're all that's left. But before that, you want to experience the pleasure of purpose and fulfillment in life. Mark Twain said, **"to get the full value of joy, you must have somebody to divide it with."** That is why we celebrate creativity publicly in the form of performances and exhibitions. When I teach art at school to elementary children, an important part of the lesson is the "gallery walk" at the end. This is where we all look at each other's work, praise it and evaluate it and thereby validate the creations and artists alike. Many schools have art evenings and performances to show off their children's work. When we grow up, this purpose of life becomes increasingly forgotten. Today, it seems there are fewer opportunities to share our creativity publicly than we once had. Wouldn't it be nice to change that?

D) Creative benefits

The final benefit of exercising creativity must be the most obvious. If you practice creativity then you will become better at it! If you are wondering why creativity itself is so important then you need to read on to Chapter 3.

Brain-Training Benefits – Summary

- Nearly all adults want to improve their brain health.

- The brain is a muscle that grows with exercise.

- Plasticity is competitive – different skills compete to use parts of your brain.

- Visualization and imagination alone can help you learn a skill.

- Creative exercises have no correct answer.

- Benefits of creativity include:

  - Health benefits

  - Happiness and wellbeing

  - Purpose and fulfillment

  - Creative benefits

- Using your brain to be cognitively active helps build your cognitive reserve which can help against diseases that attack the brain.

- Creative art therapies are increasingly being used to help with mental health, chronic illness, head injuries, physical and developmental disabilities.

- Creativity can relieve stress and make you happy.

- Creativity is a fundamental human purpose.

Chapter 3

Creativity Has Never Been More Important

What is creativity?

Before discussing why creativity is so important, we should first understand what it is. I like the simple definition that education-alist and renowned creativity expert Sir Ken Robinson uses:[32]

> **"Creativity** is an **original idea** that has **value."**

There are therefore two key parts that must be gone through in every creative process:

- **Generating ideas** – I refer to this later as Creative Strength; and
- **Determining which ideas are original and have value** and therefore are worth pursuing – I refer to this later as Creative Stamina.

An original idea by itself is not necessarily creative. If I said we should all keep balloons as pets, it might be an original idea, but one with no value. Or conversely, after a quick search, it

turns out that people have actually started making balloons in the shape of pets.[33] They've attached little legs so the balloons "walk" just off the ground and children love them! So then maybe the idea does have value but obviously it's not original if someone else is already doing it.

There is significant overlap between creativity and innovation but innovation can be distinguished from creativity in that it involves the **implementation** of a creative idea.

Amazingly most books on creativity discuss how to be more creative without discussing why! It may be that the benefits of creativity are just assumed but the problem with this is that while there will always be a solid core of devotees to creativity, everyone else misses out on understanding why it is so important to them. Here are the main reasons why we all need creativity now, more than ever.

Work in the 21st century

In the current climate, it seems like getting a job is as hard as it's ever been. Stories are always told of hundreds of overqualified applicants applying for a single position. The first hurdle to overcome is having a resume good enough to get noticed and compete with the best out there. There are a number of online sites that list active adjectives to include in your resume to help you obtain an amazing career.

As you read the list on the following page, imagine that you are making a decision about hiring a new employee. Assume that these qualities are all true. Would you hire this person?

Attributes:

Diligent	Reliable	Conscientious
Organized	Determined	Skillful
Industrious	Methodical	Hard-working
Self-starter	Persistent	Attentive
Proactive	Loyal	Dynamic
Passionate	Motivated	Trustworthy
Energetic	Consistent	Team-player

It's an impressive list. Many people would be delighted to have all these qualities or to be able to hire someone with them. There is, however, one problem.

I've just described an ant!

Read the list again and notice how these are all qualities of ants. **Who wants to be an ant?!** There is no doubt that ants are mightily impressive creatures, but for them, creativity, individuality, self-expression and imagination are not relevant or necessary parts of their life. One reason for this is that there is no need for them to be. Ant colonies replicate highly successful and efficient societies that have been developed and refined over millions of years. Their existence is not threatened in any significant way. Furthermore, the ant's whole life is essentially sacrificed for the greater good of the colony. Such an existence is fundamentally incompatible with what it means to be human where every individual is entitled to choose their own existence and to make their own meaningful life.

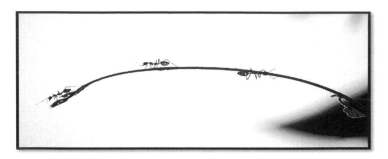

This dilemma was actually portrayed in the movie *Antz*. The hero – Z, was an anxious ant voiced by Woody Allen who wanted to be different to all the others. But your real life shouldn't make you feel like a neurotic Woody Allen character just for wanting to be different!

The Creative Age

In his book, *A Whole New Mind*, Dan Pink (no relation) has dubbed the 21st century the Conceptual Age where creators are the main characters.[34] He called the 20th Century the Information Age when it was sufficient to have a good education to get a good job and survive comfortably. But now there are computers, robots and a pool of very cheap, talented, workers in developing countries that can do knowledge-based jobs at a fraction of the cost. A 2013 Oxford University study found that nearly half of all jobs in the US are at risk of being computerized in the next 20 years![35] The US Department of Labor has found that on average, in the first 10 years of working, young adults have already held over seven jobs.[36] Jobs for life have gone forever. The good news, however, is that jobs which involve more creative skills are less likely to be taken over by computers in the future. A recent study by Nesta, a UK innovation charity, estimated that 86% of US workers in highly creative jobs were at no or low risk of losing their jobs in the future to automation. Instead, computers tend to complement these professions by making creative skills more productive.[37]

There is no turning back from here. The pace of change is now faster than ever before and continually accelerating. One study showed that in 2011, compared to 25 years before, people were receiving five times as much information and producing 200 times as much.[38] **Welcome to the Creative Age!**

Creativity in education

One consequence of living in the Creative Age is that **when a five-year-old enters Kindergarten today, we simply have no idea exactly what world they will find when they finish their education,** and even less so by the time they retire around 2080. One estimate is that two thirds of children that graduate from school will work in careers that did not exist when they started 15 years earlier![39] We need to be more creative than ever before so that we can adapt to change, add value and compete in the world. It is therefore time that the role of creativity is properly recognized, especially in education. The problem to date is simply explained by brain researcher Charles Limb: **"We are putting creativity into the category of entertainment instead of education. And that's a mistake."**[40]

Eminent academics have called for creativity to play a central role in our education systems. Sir Ken Robinson insists that **"creativity is as important in education as literacy."**[41] Harvard Professor Howard Gardner asserts that **"Educational systems that catalyze imagination and creativity will be the winners."**[42] Thankfully, there is some evidence that these calls are starting to be recognized. The P21 Partnership for 21st Century Learning lists Creativity as one of the four key skills for this century.[43] One could argue that the other three key skills identified (Critical Thinking, Collaboration, and Communication) are connected to creativity too and are useful for being creative, as we will see later on. Similarly, a 2009 survey of OECD (Organization for Economic Cooperation and Development) countries found that 15 of them explicitly identified "creativity and innovation" as a 21st-century skill that is incorporated into their education systems.[44]

Organizations in the 21st century

Creativity is not only necessary for individuals. Creativity is necessary for organizations and corporations too. 200 years ago during the Industrial Revolution or 100 years ago when the Ford Factory revolutionized industry with its assembly lines, a corporation could be dominant for decades.

Today, top executives fear a competitor with a completely different business model entering their industry and achieving market dominance in no time. Some call this the "Uber syndrome."[45] Uber has revolutionized cab rides around the world. Customers download an app to their phone and can find a driver to take them where they want. Anyone can apply to be a driver and use their own car. Uber provides the technological piece, connects the customer and driver and monitors the service provided. But the most astonishing thing is that the value of Uber exceeds that of all the car rental companies combined, even though it's just an app and it's only seven years old.[46] As the *2015 IBM Global C-Suite Report* states, **"A few years ago, [companies] could see the competition coming. Today, the competition's often invisible until it's too late."**[47]

One problem that all organizations must always face is how to improve. Gary Hamel, a well-known management guru has said, **"Most companies are built for continuous improvement, not discontinuous innovation."**[48] It means that the danger for existing companies is that they look for small, incremental improvements from their existing position rather than big changes. A good example of this is Kodak who produced the film that used to be put in cameras. They actually developed the technology for digital photography but decided not to pursue it. Now, of course, everyone carries around a digital camera in their phone while a few years ago, Kodak filed for bankruptcy protection. Continuous improvement was their downfall. It is no surprise then that in 2010, a global study by IBM of 1,500 CEOs revealed that **the most valuable leadership skill was creativity.**[49]

Lifelong Learning

These new approaches to education and work, combined with a longer life expectancy and a faster changing world, are giving rise to an inevitable phenomenon. It is no longer sufficient to front load our lives with education. **To thrive in our future world, you will have to be a lifelong learner.** A college degree is no longer enough. Singapore now awards adults learning credits that they can use throughout their working lives.[50] One of the key skills for being able to adapt to new situations and continue learning throughout life is creativity. The 2015 Nesta study estimated that currently, 21% of US jobs are highly creative.[51] The future depends not on everyone becoming an artist or musician, but rather on people in all careers using their creativity to adapt, learn, create and solve problems.

Solving humanity's problems

Finally, there is one last, massive reason why we need creativity. We are faced today with many global problems, on a level that has never been witnessed in previous human existence. There are now well over seven billion people on earth. 1 in 9 people is malnourished.[52] 1 in 10 people (not all the same) does not have access to clean water.[53] Climate change is occurring. Fossil fuels are running out. Scientists have started to label the period we are living in as a new geological time period – the Anthropocene (meaning the Age of Man) - because we are altering our planet so much and so fast. What chance do we have tackling any of these problems without creativity?

Over 200 years ago Thomas Malthus predicted that when overpopulation occurred, much of it would be wiped out by war, famine, and disease. So far he's been proven wrong, but perhaps only because he underestimated human creativity. For example, one clever invention that is helping with the world's water supply problem is the Hippo Water Roller Project.[54] The Hippo Roller is a giant plastic drum that can be placed on its side and rolled using a handle to and from the water source. It enables the user to carry up to five times more water than normal. So far it has been used in over 20 countries.

One of the great things about creativity is that any human can exercise it, no matter where they are, who they are, or what their condition. Creativity got us where we are today and it will be absolutely essential for getting us to wherever we go tomorrow.

Creativity Has Never Been More Important – Summary

- Creativity is an original idea that has value.

- Creativity is what distinguishes us from ants!

- The 21st Century is the Creative Age.

- Computers, robots and cheaper labor elsewhere force us to be creative.

- Change is happening faster than ever before and the only way to adapt is by being creative.

- Education must teach and emphasize creative skills.

- Organizations need to be creative and innovative and not just make incremental improvements.

- Everyone needs to be a lifelong learner.

- Creativity is needed to solve the unprecedented problems and challenges facing us in the world now.

Part 2

Welcome To Brainarium

Brainarium is a place to exercise and practice your creative thinking, just like you exercise your physical fitness in a gym. When you join a gym, the members of staff there assess your current health and advise you on how to use the equipment safely. We will do the same for creativity in Part 2.

Chapter 4

Creative Assessment

When you join a gym, you might take a fitness assessment to assess your current level of fitness and to see what you need to work on. This chapter includes a Creative Assessment for you to take before you enter Brainarium.

But before you start, I want to give you a warning. **There is no such thing as a true, objective test of creativity!** This is because creativity is subjective and has no right answers. So why bother?

One reason is that it is possible to examine your attitude to creativity and it may be helpful to identify factors which you believe are holding you back from being creative.

Another reason is that you can learn from the creative exercises. If you find yourself daunted or uninspired by some of the questions, **DO NOT WORRY**! You would not expect to start going to a gym and run a marathon straight away. Just like physical exercise, creative exercise works by trying something manageable, practicing, repeating and gradually stretching yourself until it becomes easier.

This assessment comes in 2 parts. Part 1 assesses your creative attitude. Part 2 assesses your creative responses. There are some sample answers to the Part 2 questions in Appendix 1.

Of course, there is no such thing as a correct answer to these questions. What I have tried to do though is show some of the possibilities for answering the questions and also to give a sense of what might be considered a more creative answer compared to a less creative answer.

Part 1: Creative attitude questions

Answer the ten questions below, checking the box closest to the statement that you believe in. You will quickly spot the pattern. It is not designed to be subtle! The point is to reflect on your own beliefs and try to assess accurately what your beliefs are at the moment.

		5	4	3	2	1	
1	I am creative.		✓				I am not creative.
2	Everyone is creative.		✓				Only certain types of people (e.g. artists) are creative.
3	Creativity is a skill that can be learned and improved.	✓					Creativity requires special talents.
4	I'm always coming up with new ideas.			✓			I never have ideas.
5	The world is fascinating.		✓				The world is boring.
6	Given a choice, I'd like to play and have fun.	✓					Given a choice, I'd like to work and be serious.
7	I question everything.			✓			I always do what I'm told and don't question the rules.
8	Failure is a learning opportunity.		✓				I fear failure.
9	I like to try new things.		✓				I like to do the same thing.
10	I like to learn from other people and encourage them too.		✓				I'm just fine by myself.

$$5 \times 2 = 10$$
$$4 \times 6 = 24$$
$$3 \times 2 = \underline{6}$$
$$40$$

41

IMPORTANT: These questions have nothing to do with whether or not you are a creative person. YOU ARE!! They are simply assessing how healthy your current attitude to creativity is. Add up all the points (from 1 to 5) for each question to get a total out of 50.

Results:

10-19:   Don't worry! – you're not quite there yet. Life/parents/teachers/friends/colleagues tricked you into thinking creativity wasn't for you. I'm telling you now – they're wrong! As you use Brainarium, you should start to believe in your own creativity.

20-29:   Your attitude to creativity is somewhere in the middle. Maybe you've experienced doubts or maybe you just haven't given it much thought. I spent 10 years as a lawyer and mostly forgot all about creativity! As you focus on it now, your interest and belief in it will grow.

30-39:   You're starting in a good place. As you learn more about creativity and start to exercise it more, your confidence in your own creativity should grow even stronger.

40-50:   Congratulations! You have a very healthy attitude to creativity. You enjoy the benefits of being creative and this will help you as you work out your creativity.

Having the right attitude is a critically important part of creativity as we will see in the next two chapters. Psychologists have found that the key difference between so-called creative people and less creative people can be as simple as creative people think that they are creative whereas less creative people don't think they are![55]

Part 2: Creative response questions

1. Fill in the squares below with pictures or designs. Try to be as unusual as you can.

2. In 1 minute, how many uses can you think of for a piece of chewing gum?

glue
eat it
smell it
throw it away
give it away

3. Describe what you see in the picture below:

4. In what ways are nuts and books connected?

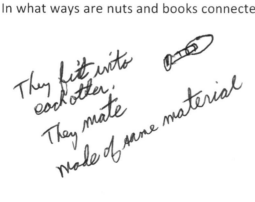

5. Complete the picture below:

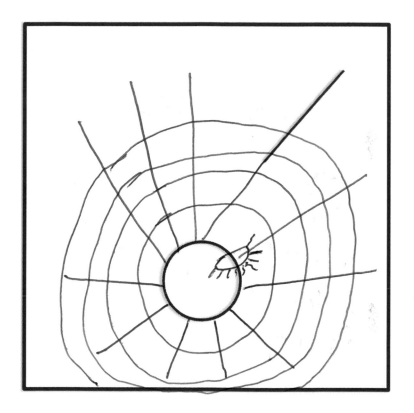

6. If money grew on trees, what would you do?

I'd chop down trees + get the money.
I'd grow trees.

7. What do you see in the picture below?

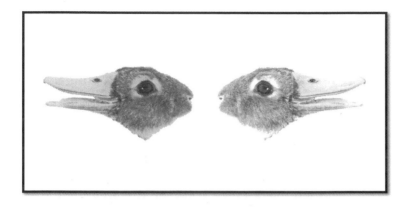

a rabbit + a duck
a deformed ~~deat~~ rabbit.
A deformed duck.
A couple.

Chapter 5

Exercising Safely

The first thing you need to learn before doing physical exercise is how to exercise safely to avoid hurting yourself. The same is true with creative exercise. **There are certain precautions you should take to avoid the risk of hurting your mental or creative attitude.** As much as possible, when making a good creative environment it is important for it to be positive rather than negative.

There are three huge dangers with potentially devastating consequences that an individual or an organization can face if they are trying to be creative: (1) Fear of Failure; (2) Fear of Judgment; and (3) Lack of Freedom. Often it is easier to identify problems than to solve them. It is also often true that the correct thing to do is easier said than done. For that reason, after each creativity-threatening danger listed below, I have offered a simple mantra which can be read, spoken aloud or reflected upon at times of difficulty to help overcome these dangers and keep your mind in the right place for creating.

1) Fear of failure

The first danger a person can face if they want to be creative is the fear of failure. Creative success rarely comes from the first attempt at something. Every famous, successful person seemingly has a tale of hardship, failure, and adversity at some point in their lives. Billionaire Sir James Dyson, the inventor of the Dyson bagless vacuum cleaner, spent 15 years and 5,126 failed attempts before he got his invention right.[56] Don't fear failure and don't give up!

This lesson is important for organizations too. It is not possible to have a creative environment if people fear failure or if the organization itself fears failure. This often explains the reason why organizations pursue incremental change rather than the discontinuous innovation referred to in Chapter 3. Especially when an organization is successful, it seems much safer to keep doing the same thing and make small improvements. But the problem now is that historic success and market position can be wiped out very quickly.

There is another reason why it is so important to allow failure and to allow people to make mistakes. It is one of the best ways to learn, experiment and refine new developments. One of the most dramatic examples of failure must be the story of Jack Welch, former CEO of General Electric and widely recognized as one of the greatest leaders of the 20th century. Early on in his career at GE, he blew up a plastics factory! It's hard to think of a more catastrophic mistake that you could make at work. The next day he was sent to Connecticut to explain himself, but instead of losing his job he was asked what he thought had happened and if he could fix it.[57] The key point, which GE understood, is that everybody makes mistakes but it is important to learn from them. If GE had fired Jack Welch, in the long term the corporation might never have had the subsequent success it had. Organizations therefore have to allow people to make mistakes.

Mantra for Exercising Safely (1):

- *Failure is part of the process.*

- *It happens to everyone.*

- *I will learn from my mistakes.*

2) Fear of judgment

While being creative is a fundamental human trait, so is the need to be accepted. Therefore one of the hardest situations in life is where we feel that anyone can or might judge us. Criticism can be hard to take, even when it is constructively given and well-meaning. The fear of not being good enough is a common one, even among highly successful people. Public speaking is often listed as a top fear that people have and one of the main reasons for this is that a speaker is in the spotlight being judged by their audience. One of the main ways to allay this fear is to point out to the speaker that the audience actually wants them to succeed. No one wants to go and listen to a boring speech! The audience is on the same side as the speaker.

Creativity can draw lessons from this. It is important to find your audience – that is to say, the people who will appreciate and be receptive to your ideas and creativity. Unfortunately, this may not always be the situation you find yourself in. Sometimes your creations will be judged and maybe not everyone will want you to succeed. This could be because of something as random as differences in personal taste or because of something more sinister such as office politics. Depending on your role, there are two things you can do here. As the creator, develop a thicker skin so that you don't fear other people's judgment and certainly don't let it stop your creativity. As a potential evaluator of someone else's creativity or ideas, be sensitive when giving your feedback and if at all possible, be sincerely encouraging and enthusiastic. **The power of thoughtful, sincere encouragement is amazing.**

Social media offers many exciting opportunities to connect instantly and spread ideas with people around the world but its amazing ability to give your creations exposure can also be harmful. It is easy for other people to "troll" or criticize, especially because they can often do this relatively anonymously. This means that they're often not held accountable and they can make a sport out of such a nasty habit. It seems evident that the more people that see your work, the higher the chances that someone won't like it. Again, the only real solution (other than to run away from social media, as some have done) is to ignore it and enjoy the praise from those that appreciate your work and ideas.

One of the most wonderful examples of turning conventional judgment on its head is the story of The Really Terrible Orchestra or RTO, who proudly proclaim themselves "the cream of Edinburgh's musically disadvantaged."[58] The RTO is the brainchild of author Alexander McCall Smith who realized that children have fun playing instruments in orchestras but that this pleasure is denied to adults unless you can play music to a certain standard. The RTO is comprised of amateur musicians who want to play music but who have been prevented from so doing, perhaps because of a lack of talent. Accessibility is very much prioritized over ability and the musicians have great fun expressing their creativity this way. Perhaps more surprisingly, the RTO has been a hit with audiences too. The RTO has performed to sell-out audiences in London and New York!

Mantra for Exercising Safely (2):

- *I understand that not everyone will like my ideas or creations.*

- *I will not waste time worrying about unfair or nasty criticism.*

- *I will appreciate positive feedback and encouragement and give the same to others whenever possible.*

3) Lack of freedom

The third big danger is that you have a lack of freedom to be creative which can sometimes manifest itself as a fear of other people or circumstances controlling what you are able to do.

If you are creating by yourself and feel that you have a lack of freedom, the first step is to analyze what is holding you back. It could be money, time, distractions or something else (including the fear of failure and fear of judgment mentioned above). The solution will depend on the obstacle but could be to:

- Save money to allow you to pursue a creative dream;

- Block out a sacred time for creating;

- Find that special place that puts you in the right mood to be creative; or

- Avoid the naysayers who suck your creative energy out of you.

It can be difficult when you work for an organization and are tasked with producing creative ideas and yet the organization itself gives little freedom to its people. I remember with a mixture of amusement and bemusement the time when my law firm asked me to be part of a focus group generating ideas about what the law firm of the future would look like. As the brainstorming session commenced, my first idea was that one day lawyers might be able to choose the hours they worked. The idea was immediately shot down by the facilitator who remarked that such an idea could never happen! At that point, my enthusiasm for the session ended because I presumed that the firm had no real interest in brainstorming for the future. Instead, this was just a box-checking exercise for the human resources department to say that they had consulted lawyers about the future of the firm. As we will see later, the facilitator's attitude and words fundamentally misunderstood brainstorming and creativity, but it was quite consistent with just looking for small, incremental changes.

Psychologists have studied creativity in children and in particular, noticed that the following behaviors hindered their ability to be creative:[59]

- Judging them;

- Telling them exactly how to do things;

- Putting too much pressure on them;

- Constantly watching them; and

- Putting them in a win/lose situation.

How would you feel in these situations? These are exactly the same behaviors that could hinder an adult's freedom to be creative. There is always the potential for conflict between what an organization describes as its culture and what is needed to foster creativity. When employees are told how to behave and react down to the tiniest detail there is less opportunity for them to be creative.

Another issue to be wary of is a culture that inadvertently hinders creativity. An example of this might be where employees are rewarded not to question anything and essentially be "yes men" to their bosses. The TV show *Undercover Boss* regularly demonstrates that front line workers are full of ideas about how to improve their organizations but these ideas usually go unnoticed until the CEO happens by chance to hear them because he or she is undercover.

One possible answer to this is to incorporate being creative into the culture. Google was famous for this with its *"20% time"* – the idea that employees were free to spend one day a week working on their own projects. Some major successes came out of this such as Gmail. Even if the concept was never formally set in stone and even if the time didn't necessarily equate to 20%,[60] the principle is still of great value in promoting creativity.

Another solution is to think about ways to capture people's creativity. Employee surveys and feedback, especially on joining and leaving could be especially useful, but only if the employees feel truly free to speak their minds. Are there suggestions boxes and incentives for good ideas? Are employees given a fresh stimulus to enhance their creativity such as the opportunity to spend time in different locations or departments?

Mantra for Exercising Safely (3):

- *I will give myself the freedom I need to be creative.*

- *If necessary, I will use my creativity to help get the freedom I need to be creative!*

- *I will not prevent others from being creative.*

Exercising Safely – Summary

- The 3 dangers to creativity are fear of failure, fear of judgment and lack of freedom.

- Everyone makes mistakes. Learn from them and don't give up!

- Find your audience and encourage others.

- Give yourself the freedom to be creative.

Complete Mantra for Exercising Safely

- *Failure is part of the process.*

- *It happens to everyone.*

- *I will learn from my mistakes.*

- *I understand that not everyone will like my ideas or creations.*

- *I will not waste time worrying about unfair or nasty criticism.*

- *I will appreciate positive feedback and encouragement and give the same to others whenever possible.*

- *I will give myself the freedom I need to be creative.*

- *If necessary, I will use my creativity to help get the freedom I need to be creative!*

- *I will not prevent others from being creative.*

Chapter 6

A Creative Diet For A Creative Life

A good diet is an important part of being healthy. Likewise, **your creative diet is important for your creative health**. What should you consume or surround yourself with for a healthy, creative life? This chapter will present a number of useful tips for a creative diet.

There are three main areas to focus on and they can be remembered by thinking APE! This stands for:

A = Attitude
P = People
E = Environment

We will consider each of these in turn.

1) Attitude

The correct attitude builds on the advice from Chapter 5. Certainly, it is essential not to fear failure or judgment. But having the correct creative attitude requires positive focus as well.

Key Tips

- **Just start**

  Even the greatest creative geniuses can feel uninspired. One of their secrets is that they work anyway, even if they haven't been hit with "creative inspiration." Once you have started something it becomes easier to develop.

- **The more you practice, the easier it gets**

  This is true of all exercise and especially creativity.

- **There are no "right" (or "wrong") answers**

  From our earliest years, we are taught the "right" way to do things. We often crave the validation of a correct answer, as much as our teachers encourage us to give one. But creativity is different. There are no "right" or "wrong" answers. Just have a go and enjoy it!

- **Go for quantity**

  If you wanted to win the lottery, would you rather have one ticket or 1,000 tickets? Creativity is a numbers game. The more ideas you have, the more you increase your chances of producing a great creation. Behind every creative idea that succeeded are many more ideas that failed.

- **Have fun!**

  If you are enjoying what you do then it will not seem like work. Children are experts in having fun and look how wonderfully creative they are. (Chapter 9 goes into more detail about this.) Humor is also very creative, so why not see if you can bring some humor to the table?

- **Follow your excitement**
  If something interests you then go in that direction as you may be more alert to opportunities that could arise.

- **Be open-minded**
  Creativity involves original ideas. Original ideas will be different to previous ideas so open your mind to new possibilities in order to end up in different places to normal. This applies both to your thought processes but also more literally. If you traveled somewhere new, what new ideas might you come up with?

- **Build on other ideas**
  Although you are trying to find original ideas, you do not have to start from scratch. It is unusual to find an idea or invention that is completely original in every way. Most ideas build on previous ideas of other people. Look around for inspiration from others and build on it.

- **Can you break the rules?**
  I'm not advocating illegality but one of the constraints on creativity is thinking that certain rules have to be obeyed. What do they say? What don't they say? How can you interpret them? A lot of lateral thinking and problem solving involves breaking implied rules. **Remember every rule can be broken except this one.**

- **Question everything**
  This is a healthy mental activity even when you are not using it for creativity. There may be all sorts of implicit

assumptions that can only be challenged if you ask lots of questions.

- **Take risks**
  One way to test the water with a new idea is to use the *"Ready, Fire, Aim"* approach. This is an approach to get an idea to market sooner. Ideas are rarely perfect first time and usually need refining. Instead of spending too long trying to get an idea perfect ("aim") before unleashing it, get the idea out ("fire") and then refine it later.

- **Welcome failure**
  And learn from it! See Chapter 5 for more about this.

- **Be persistent**
  It is hard to be creative if you give up!

- **Defer judgment**
  Judgment is the key second stage of the creative process (see Chapter 10 – Creative Stamina). However, you do not want to be judgmental when you are first coming up with ideas, as it could stop the flow of ideas, or tempt you to pursue only safe ideas.

- **Enjoy the ride**
  The process can be as rewarding as the outcome. Creating can give you joy and satisfaction.

2) People

Creativity can certainly be practiced alone. There are however many benefits to enlisting the help of other people and sometimes you might be required to be creative when working as part of a team.

Key Tips

- **Work with someone else**
  Many great ideas come from partnerships and collabora-
  tions. Two heads can be better than one because you can
  bounce ideas off each other when brainstorming. Try
  working with someone else when you have the chance.

- **Learn from experts**
  One of the best ways to master a new skill is to learn from
  experts. Study how other creative people work and copy
  their methods (but not their actual ideas!).

- **Seek diversity**
  One of the major ways to be creative is to consider different
  perspectives (see Chapter 7). If you can seek out and
  surround yourself with diverse people, you will have richer
  experiences to draw from when using stimuli to create
  ideas.

- **Appreciate multiple intelligences**
  Individuals work and learn in different ways. Some people
  are visual learners, some auditory and some kinesthetic
  (which means they like to learn by doing). Understanding
  your preferred method of learning can be helpful but it may
  also present an opportunity to be stimulated in a different
  way to normal. For example, if you always read books, why
  not listen to an audio book? If you are working with a group
  of people, try to understand the different ways in which
  people prefer to learn and work.

- **Capture other people's creativity**
  If you are responsible for other people, do you have a way
  to capture their creative ideas? For example, at work, is
  everybody encouraged to speak, or do secretaries or

cleaners not have a voice? **People are more observant and creative when faced with a fresh stimulus.** Do you capture the ideas of people when they join (or visit) your organization? A new employee is likely to tread carefully, not wanting to offend their new boss, but as they go through their induction, they're also likely to see straight away what could be improved. Do you have a suggestions box for employees to submit ideas? Do you have a system of small rewards in place for such ideas (or bigger rewards if an idea revolutionizes an organization)?

- **Appreciate other people's creativity**
  This reflects the golden rule – treat others as you wish to be treated. Not only is it good to help and encourage people (not to mention a fundamental principle from our Declaration of Creativity) but you are also likely to see the favor returned. By appreciating creativity, you also receive the therapeutic benefits of enjoying beautiful, clever, marvelous works of art or ideas.

- **Avoid negative people!**
  We discussed the dangers of negativity in Chapter 5. Motivational speaker Jim Rohn says that we are the average of the five people we spend the most time with.[61] There is no room for negative people in your life!

3) Environment

It is very hard to be creative if you do not have the right environment. This was touched on when we looked at lack of freedom in Chapter 5.

Key Tips

- **Find your inspiration place**

  Where do you have most of your ideas? Is it walking in the woods or taking a shower? Find your inspiration place and go there when you need to think creatively. Research by Scott Kaufmann and Hansgrohe (the shower manufacturer) found that 72% of people experience new ideas in the shower. Indeed, some have showers for the sole reason of generating ideas![62]

- **Capture your ideas**

  Wherever your inspiration place is, you will need to have a way to capture your ideas at that moment (or soon afterward before they leave you). Keep an idea notebook or a voice recorder (or smartphone) to hand. Ideas are like dreams and they can disappear quickly so make sure you don't lose them!

- **Collect ideas and other stimuli**

  It is not just your own ideas that you should collect. If you see an interesting idea, picture or article, you should collect that too. It may be useful in the future, particularly as a stimulus for generating more ideas or as something you can build upon. Examples of things you could collect include photos, magazine articles, newspaper clippings and Dr. Seuss books. Online sites such as Pinterest are useful ways to collect and find further interesting ideas by topic.

- **Try something new**

  It is easy to become a creature of habit. There is comfort in familiar things. Habits are also necessary for our brains to remain efficient. We could not live our lives successfully if every tiny action required decision-making. BUT, new ideas feed off new experiences. We saw in Chapter 2 that this is literally how our brains grow. So trying new experiences is a great way to keep the brain active and healthy and to stimulate new ideas. Which of the following could you change or try new versions of?

- Food and drink

- Work

- TV, news, books

- Music and radio

- Route traveled to work or other places

- Vacation destinations

- Hobbies and recreation

- Friends!

- **Make time**
  Part of recognizing the importance of creativity is to make the time to do it. This allows you the chance to be creative without other conflicts and demonstrates to yourself (and others) the value you are placing on it.

- **Take a break**
  Unfortunately, creativity does not always flow like water out of a tap. As with any form of work or exercise, regular breaks are important. Set a time limit for how long you will focus on creativity if that is helpful.

- **Look to nature**
  The beauty, diversity, and creativity of nature are truly astounding. Whenever possible, get outside, appreciate it, and take inspiration from it.

- **Be observant**
  This is important when outside appreciating nature, but also in any situation. In a new environment, look carefully and ask what you notice with your senses. In a very familiar situation, ask what you can notice that you have never noticed before.

- **Travel**
  Travel is a subset of trying something new, but I mention it separately because it must be one of the most stimulating experiences possible. The further you travel from home, especially abroad, the more likely it is that people do things completely differently to what you are used to. Such experiences can provide many new ideas and have been the basis of many successful business ideas. Even if you cannot get abroad, a city often has very distinct areas reflecting different cultures. Failing that, there are always document-aries, books, and the internet.

A Creative Diet For A Creative Life – Summary

Attitude

- Just start
- The more you practice, the easier it gets
- There are no "right" (or "wrong") answers
- Go for quantity
- Have fun!
- Follow your excitement
- Be open-minded
- Build on other ideas
- Can you break the rules?
- Question everything
- Take risks
- Welcome failure
- Be persistent
- Defer judgment
- Enjoy the ride

People

- Work with someone else
- Learn from experts
- Seek diversity
- Appreciate multiple intelligences
- Capture other people's creativity
- Appreciate other people's creativity
- Avoid negative people!

Environment

- Find your inspiration place
- Capture your ideas
- Collect ideas and other stimuli
- Try something new
- Make time
- Take a break
- Look to nature
- Be observant
- Travel

Part 3

Brainarium:
Workout Routines

Having seen the necessity of creativity and understood how to exercise safely, it is finally time to start exercising creativity. I have divided the exercises into two key stages: Creative Strength and Creative Stamina.

Remember the definition of creativity: **Creativity is an original idea that has value.**

- **Creative Strength** exercises help generate ideas.
- **Creative Stamina** exercises help evaluate whether the ideas are original and have value.

The key differences between the Creative Strength and Creative Stamina stages are shown in the table below.

Creative Strength	Creative Stamina
Generating ideas.	Evaluating and judging ideas. Are the ideas original? Do they have value?
Divergent thinking (exploring many possible solutions).	Convergent thinking (narrowing down possibilities).
No correct answers – anything goes!	Looking for a most correct or suitable answer.
• Different Perspectives (Chapter 7) • Making Connections (Chapter 8) • Play and Imagination (Chapter 9)	• Judge, evaluate, compare ideas. • Reduce, eliminate ideas. • Refine, develop, improve ideas. (all Chapter 10)

The Creative Strength exercises have been further split into three chapters, each one dealing with a major creative theme. Clearly, there is some overlap between the themes and some of the exercises, but the advantage to breaking creativity into themes is that it allows you to focus on your creative fitness and to remember more easily how to be creative in any situation.

Chapter 7

Creative Strength: Different Perspectives

One of the major themes of creativity and creative exercises is to consider different perspectives. Often, we get so used to viewing the world through the same perspective (usually of our own daily lives) that it can be hard to appreciate how differently others might perceive it or how many different ways there might be to approach a problem. In this chapter, we will consider three alternative approaches to considering different perspectives:

- **Come from a different direction**
- **Think like someone else**
- **How can I change it?**

1) Come from a different direction

There is a well-known parable from India about a group of blind men and an elephant. A group of blind men was led to an elephant and each one was asked to feel a part of it and describe what he felt. What the men said depended on which part of the elephant each of them was touching. Unsurprisingly, their answers were completely different from each other (a rope, a pillar, a branch and so on). In some versions of this story, the men then got angry with each other because each one was convinced that he alone was correct and that the others were wrong. There are many metaphors from this story but the metaphor for creativity is that **you can use different perspectives to get very different results.**

Exercise 1
Turn It Upside Down

There is normally a conventional way of looking at an object or an issue. What happens if you turn it upside down?

This is an opportunity to notice things you may not have noticed before or you may find that you now feel differently about a situation. There is no reason why the "upside down earth" map is not just as valid as conventional maps but it seems strange to view it this way. Do you feel differently about where you live when you look at this map?

A well-known drawing exercise is to copy a picture upside down. The reason for this is that when you look at the picture the correct way up, your brain makes assumptions and presumes knowledge about the picture that may not be true. These natural reactions then interfere with your ability to see  the actual picture in front of you. When you turn it upside down, the brain can see more clearly where the lines are and can focus on copying them. The same can be true for creative ideas and problem solving.

Key Questions:

- What different angles can I look at something from? (Up, down, sideways etc.)

- What looks different?

- What had I not noticed before?

- What is surprising?

- What ideas does this new perspective give me?

Exercise 2

Change The Assumptions (or Breaking Down The Brick Wall)

Most situations have a series of assumptions and those assumptions can often form a brick wall that we cannot break down. Sometimes we are aware of this but at other times we may not even be conscious of the barriers that these assumptions can form.

But maybe these assumptions are not necessary or maybe they could be changed. Once upon a time, there was an assumption that a bookseller had to sell books in a bookstore. Then Jeff Bezos changed that assumption and founded Amazon so that people could buy books online.

Two assumptions in a business might be that you want to give good customer service or that you want to make a profit. Those assumptions can be turned on their head. What if the object was to lose money or to offend customers? By considering these questions important ideas can arise. For example, if a company wanted to lose money, it could give all its products away. But as you start to think about that idea, there may be value to it. KIND Snacks is one example of a successful organization that believes "there's more to business than just profit"[63] and they give away large numbers of their snacks and granola bars both to the public and as donations to other organizations.

Key Questions:

- What are the assumptions?

- Are those assumptions necessary?

- How could those assumptions be changed?

- What is the opposite of those assumptions?

- What ideas or results follow from the changed assumptions?

- What is the potential value in the new ideas or results?

Exercise 3
Back To Front

We saw in Chapter 3 the dangers of incremental change. One of the reasons why incremental change is such a temptation is that it is natural to start at where you are and think about what you can change. But it is sometimes futile. Imagine an asteroid hurtling toward you while you try to decide what color to repaint the house! To look at the bigger picture, it is helpful to take a step back and consider the end goal and then consider the steps toward it.

The bigger the ambition, the greater the chance of creativity. It is well known that if an organization sets a target of 5% growth there is a risk that it will meet that target, but nothing higher because the goal was the target and nothing more. It can be more inspirational to work toward big goals than small ones. Fun can even be had with this exercise by posing ridiculous targets e.g. how could my idea reach everyone in the world? Remember a key part of Creative Strength is not to dismiss silly ideas.

Key Questions:

- What is my end goal?

- What does success (for this project) look like?

- Working backward, what steps would need to be taken to get there?

- What feasible ideas come out of this?

2) Think like someone else

An effective way to be creative or to solve problems is to abandon your initial approach and rethink the problem in a different way. The famous thinker Edward de Bono called this **"lateral thinking."** A particularly effective way of thinking laterally is to think like someone else. The following "8 Geese Problem" demonstrates this idea nicely.

Find the missing value:

0 = 1

82 = 2

96 = 2

bad = 3

6 cats = 2

2 Dogs = 3

6 geese = 5

8 GEESE = ?

This type of problem may well appeal to certain people more than others, especially those who like patterns and logical thinking. There are a number of obvious places to start thinking. Does the number of characters or digits affect the answer? Is it connected to the value of the numbers or a perceived value of characters e.g. a=1, b=2 and so on? Is the difference between numbers and letters significant? What difference do capitals make? Is there some pattern involving adding and subtracting from the numbers or letters?

Typically, when faced with this problem for the first time, an adult tries all the obvious answers and gets increasingly perplexed as they are continually told they are wrong. Moreover, further examples tend to confuse rather than help the puzzler as their potential solutions become ever more convoluted. After 15 minutes of frustration when I first saw this puzzle, I was given a clue that finally helped me: "When engineering graduates looked at this puzzle, they couldn't solve it. But a group of kindergarteners solved it very quickly." For some, that clue may be no help either! What it is hinting at, though, is that the answer is a simple one rather than a complicated one. To solve it, you have to think like a kindergartner, which usually eliminates most of the complicated ideas you were having. What does a five-year-old know and what would they notice in the above puzzle? Have another go at the puzzle now. The answer is at the end of this chapter.* Changing perspectives to think very differently gave all the help necessary to solve a problem that was seemingly impossible.

Exercise 4
What Would "X" Do?

The most obvious way to think like someone else is to imagine what they would do in a given situation. The person imagined could be famous (e.g. Elvis Presley, the Queen) or a family member, friend or colleague. It could be a specific person or a type of person (e.g. a child). They can be alive or dead (e.g. George Washington). The exercise is then to insert that chosen person into a situation and imagine what they would do or what the situation would be like based on their character traits, views, skills, experience and so on.

For example:

- What would America be like if Oprah Winfrey was President?

- How would school be different if the principal was a child?

As with other exercises, it does not matter if the person chosen is seemingly absurd. The point is to brainstorm the person and then the situation and see what ideas you have.

If a child were principal...		
Traits of a child	**Jobs of a principal**	**Ideas**
• Energetic • Fun • Like to play • Messy • Loud • Run • Accident-prone	• Runs school • Sets schedule • Responsible for safety • Speaks to parents • Manages budget • Hires teachers	• More focus on recess • Make school fun • Pad corners, furniture so it is safe to run around the place! • Meetings with parents have to happen on the playground while playing

Exercise 5
Different Roles

This exercise works especially well if you have a team or group of people working on an idea. Each person takes a different, defined role and focuses on the issue from that perspective only. A classic example of this is Edward de Bono's idea of *Six Thinking Hats*.[64] A group splits into six different roles (or "colored hats") each with a different focus. Blue focuses on the process, white on the facts, red on the feelings, green on creativity, yellow on the positives and lastly black is cautious or judgmental. It should be noted that while the role played by the black hat is a necessary one, it often hinders idea creation, which is why I have suggested leaving idea evaluation to the second stage of the creative process (see Chapter 10 – Creative Stamina).

There are many alternative ways of doing this exercise. For example, you could assign roles based on different:

- Jobs

- Abilities

- Age/gender/race/religion

- Attitudes/moods

- Wealth

- Nationality

It is up to you how practical you want the roles assigned to be. For example, if you owned a shop, you might want people taking the role of a customer, the boss, a shop assistant, a parent, a cleaner and a passer-by. But you could pick anyone (see "What Would "X" Do?" above) if you wanted more out-of-the-box ideas.

Key Questions:

- What different roles shall we choose?

- What natural diversity and expertise exists in the group already?

- For each role, what is that character's motivation?

- What does it feel like to be them?

- What would their concerns be?

- What are common themes between characters? What are the differences?

Exercise 6
Expert Help

There may be times when you recognize that you need the help or ideas of others. That is fine! **Collaboration is one of the best ways to be creative.** An obvious place to start is to find out about the expertise of people you know and see if you can use it toward your idea or problem. There are other ways to find expertise, though. If you want to see what lawyers are like, go and visit a courtroom and watch a trial. Different situations and experiences are always likely to trigger new ideas.

Another idea can be to research what other people or organizations do. For example, if you want to see how other organizations come up with new ideas, you could get a group of individuals to research and report back on what Apple, Google, Amazon, and Tesla do. The research need not be a huge project. Even after 15 minutes on the internet or reading magazines, a person could find out useful information and become the "expert" on those companies. For example, a quick search of Tesla brings up a number of interesting ideas:

- Their CEO announces a grand idea before providing details, leaving others to speculate how it could be done.

- He says that their designs will be open source and not secret or patented.[65]

- He plans to have a competition for students to design key parts of the invention.[66]

One final point that comes out of this is that the more diverse your life, friends, and workplace are, the richer the experiences are that you and others can draw from to help be creative.

Key Questions:

- Which experts could help us?

- Are the experts available to us?

- Can we research what the experts do?

- How can we apply their expertise to our situation?

3) How can I change it?

Considering different perspectives has often been a way to fundamentally rethink ideas and knowledge that were previously widely accepted. What if the earth were round not flat? What if the earth traveled around the sun? These different perspectives fundamentally changed history, though they were ridiculed at first. Naturally not every different perspective will be as fundamental, but there is always the possibility of coming up with a new creative idea by thinking about how you can change an object, idea, thought or problem.

Consider birthdays. Once a year, we all celebrate the anniversary of our birthday in years. Sometimes, throughout the year, we might be aware that we just passed a half-year anniversary or that on a certain date of a month, it is an exact number of months to our next birthday. Our culture makes no attempt to acknowledge any other age milestones, which is surprising given how commercialized birthdays are and given how much people look forward to something to celebrate. Below are some key dates you may have been missing:

New Birthday Anniversary	Conventional Age**
100 months	8 years, 4 months
1,000 weeks	19 years, 9 weeks
10,000 days	27 years, 138 days
100,000 hours	11 years, 149 days
10 million minutes	19 years, 4 days
1 billion seconds	31 years, 251 days

**Approximate age, as this will be affected by leap years. If you wish to know your exact dates, you can look them up online.[67]

Before my first child was born, I learned an interesting fact. About halfway through pregnancy, a female fetus has all the eggs it will ever have. This means that even before your mother was born, the egg that would one day become you was already in existence. Given that half your genetic material comes from this egg, this means that half of you existed before your mother was born! If we think of such dates as "Egg Birthdays," we're all much older than we thought we were under conventional thinking. You can add your mother's age to yours to find out how old you are in "Egg Years." This means that I'm 27 Egg Years older than my conventional age!

When you consider different perspectives the possibilities are endless.

Exercise 7
How Many Uses?

This is a good warm-up exercise to get the brain working. Pick an object and give yourself a limited amount of time. Try to think of as many possible uses for that object as you can within the time.

For example, in five minutes, how many ways can you think of to use a paperclip? It is likely that you would start by listing actual uses such as holding paper together, but as the number of ideas increases, your creativity will come up with less obvious ideas e.g. an earring, a toothpick or a snake (if joined together with lots of other paperclips).

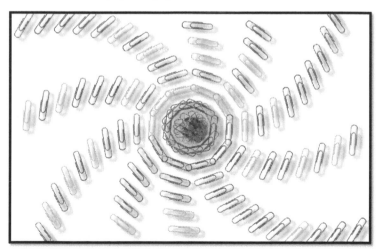

At the end of the exercise, you should have moved away from thinking of the object just in the narrow sense for which it is usually used and now have a greater sense of the possibilities for which it could be used.

Exercise 8
Break It Up

It is often easy to view things as a whole without always appreciating their component parts. A good way to understand something better is to take it apart and see what it's made of. The idea behind this exercise is that when you break something up, you may find a better or different way to put it back together. You may even find a way to add in different objects that were not previously part of it. The same principles apply to ideas and assumptions.

A good example of this is the tangram, which is a collection of seven different sized shapes that can be made into a square. When taken apart there are literally hundreds of different pictures that you can create just by rearranging the 7 shapes.

Key Questions:

- How can I take this apart?

- What is it made of? What are the parts made of?

- Can I change/replace/add/take away parts?

- Can I put it back together in a different way?

- What do I know now that I didn't know before?

- What are the advantages/disadvantages of keeping it the same?

Exercise 9
What's Missing?

Look at the box below. What do you see?

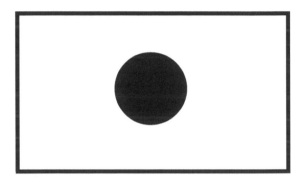

Most people would answer that they see a black dot or circle in the middle of the box. There is actually far more blank or white space around the dot within the box, yet this often goes unnoticed. We call this blank space around the object, negative space. It can often reveal as much as the object itself does (for example, see the picture below).

Just as management guru Peter Drucker said, "the most important thing in communication is hearing what isn't said," the object of this exercise is to look for what is missing or what you are not seeing. This is also a situation where diversity helps. People with different experience who think differently to you may well see things that you do not.

Key Questions:

- What is in the negative space? What am I missing?

- How does the negative space affect my understanding of the whole object (or issue)?

- What is the relationship between the negative space and the object?

- How do they affect each other?

- How can I use the negative space to be creative?

Exercise 10

SCAMPER

SCAMPER is an acronym that uses some of the ideas we have already discussed in other exercises. It was first proposed in 1953 by Alex Osborn (the man who popularized the term brainstorming) and later developed by Bob Eberle. Each letter stands for an action you can do to the object or idea and forms a useful checklist of ways to change an object or idea.

> S – Substitute
> C – Combine
> A – Adapt/Adjust
> M – Modify/Magnify
> P – Put it to another use
> E – Eliminate
> R – Reverse/Rearrange

S – Substitute

When you look at your object or idea, what could you replace? Could you substitute the whole thing or just a part?

C – Combine

What can you combine an object or idea with? Chapter 8 focuses on making connections with new things which could be combined with the original object or idea.

A – Adapt/Adjust

How can something be adapted and improved, perhaps borrowing from other ideas? What consequences and effects follow from the change?

M – Modify/Magnify

How can you change the idea and make it bigger (perhaps by adding another element to it)?

P – Put it to another use

This is like Exercise 7 (How Many Uses?).

E – Eliminate

What can you get rid of that is not necessary?

R – Reverse/Rearrange

This is like a mixture of Exercise 2 (Change the Assumptions) and Exercise 8 (Break It Up).

This checklist works both as a guide through the whole creative process with an idea or as something that could be implemented at each stage of the creative process. It is not necessary that each action is completed but rather it is a guideline to stimulate creative ideas.

* Answer to the 8 GEESE problem

The answer is 8 GEESE = 2. Each answer is counting the total number of "circles" or enclosed spaces in the letters and numbers. In this case, the number "8" has 2 enclosed spaces but none of the letters in "GEESE" do, so the answer is 2.

Creative Strength:
Different Perspectives – Summary

Come from a different direction

- Turn It Upside Down
- Change The Assumptions (Breaking Down The Brick Wall)
- Back To Front

Think like someone else

- What Would "X" Do?
- Different Roles
- Expert Help

How can I change it?

- How Many Uses?
- Break It Up
- What's Missing?
- **SCAMPER**

    S – Substitute
    C – Combine
    A – Adapt/Adjust
    M – Modify/Magnify
    P – Put it to another Use
    E – Eliminate
    R – Reverse/Rearrange

Chapter 8

Creative Strength: Making Connections

In Chapter 1, we saw the way neurons in our brain make connections to each other using synapses and how that process develops our brains. Making connections is also an important technique for being creative. The reason for this is that making a connection between two things creates a new stimulus which can help lead to new ideas which are an essential part of creativity. In this chapter, we will consider three approaches to making connections. These can be distinguished by how closely related (or unrelated) to each other the items being compared are:

- **Random Objects**
- **The Comparison**
- **The Path**

1) Random objects

Probably the greatest game of all time that requires you to make connections is *Lego*. Consider the simple 2 x 4 studded *Lego* brick. If you had six of them (as in the picture below), how many different ways do you think there are to arrange these six blocks?

People usually give answers in the thousands or maybe a million. The answer is nearly a billion! It's actually about 915 million but let's call it roughly a billion.[68] Isn't that amazing? It goes to show that there are usually many more ways of connecting things than is obvious at first. This is also a metaphor for our brains and for creativity itself. In our heads and at our fingertips we have literally millions of possibilities to be creative.

But using the idea of making connections in creativity does not just mean physically connecting things together. It means making connections in your mind between things that you would not normally connect. If the objects that are connected are more unusual, then the ideas that flow from the connection are likely to be more surprising and creative too. **You can connect anything to anything** and for that reason, a great stimulus for creativity is to make connections between random objects.

A recent example of a combination that no one could have predicted is the hugely successful computer game *Plants vs. Zombies*. Plants with weapons defend the backyard against the invading (and comical) undead. Creator George Fan wanted to produce a game that was not "too gritty" or "too sugary."[69] Now the concept is so popular and widespread, plants and zombies are an obvious connection to many people!

Exercise 11
Perfectly Random

This is the quintessential random creativity exercise. At its very simplest, pick a random word or object. Then ask how that random word or object can be connected to your focus. As you make connections (the more the better), it will help you to generate creative ideas about whatever you are focusing on.

You can pick a random word in any way you want e.g. look around and pick something you see, open a book and pick a word or ask someone to name a random object. The exercise could, by all means, work with non-random words too. The advantage of a random word though is that it is more likely to force you to be creative as you will have fewer preconceptions about how the random word is connected to your focus.

If your focus is thinking about original ways to make people happy and smile and you pick the random word "umbrella" you might think about the following:

- Umbrellas make people happy by keeping them dry.

- Umbrellas can have funny designs on them.

- Many umbrellas look the same and so does everyone that uses them on a rainy day. Note – strictly speaking this is just an observation about umbrellas rather than a "connection" to making people happy. Sometimes though, observations help and give you ideas as can be seen on the next page. Don't allow the "rules" of the exercise to stifle your creativity or that would be counter-productive!

What ideas might flow from this?

- Is there a way you could make people happy by providing them with an umbrella when they needed one?

- Given the purpose of an umbrella is to keep people dry, would people find it funny if you used a holey umbrella that made you wet (following the success of the *Ice Bucket Challenge*)?

- Could you decorate an umbrella creatively to make it funny e.g. look like an animal, paint an emoji on it, or an amusing slogan?

- Could you stand out by using an umbrella in an unusual situation, e.g. indoors? I had never thought or heard of this before I wrote it but it turns out that there is indeed a *National Open an Umbrella Indoors Day* on March 13![70]

You may or may not think these ideas are good, but the point is that they all flowed from a completely random word that would never normally have been associated with making people happy. Imagine how many more ideas you could get just by trying more random words.

Variations:

- Pick 2 (or more) random words and connect them.

- Pick a number of random words and find the odd one out.

- Pick a number of random words and show how each one could be used to improve what you are focusing on.

Exercise 12
If We Were All Bugs (or Connecting To Categories)

This exercise builds on the previous exercise by making connections with a category of objects (e.g. bugs, animals, fruit, toys, sports). Imagine that your challenge was to find a new and effective leadership style. You pick a category (e.g. bugs) and then pick a number of examples of that category (e.g. ant, spider, fly). Start by brainstorming all the things you know about those bugs. Then consider how their attributes could apply to leadership and what lessons you could learn from them.

Bugs:	Ant	Spider	Fly
Attributes	• Strong • Hard-working • Team player • Uses initiative • Decisive • Aggressive if necessary	• Calculating • Builds webs • 8 legs • Poisonous • Patient • Works alone	• Flies • Buzzes • Annoying • Dirty • Keeps trying to escape if trapped
How does this apply to leadership?	Leaders need to be strong and take decisive action, on their own if necessary.	Leaders need to plan ahead, execute their plans ruthlessly but sometimes be patient.	Leaders are not afraid to go to places where others will not go.

Bugs:	Ant	Spider	Fly
What can we learn from this type of leader?	Although the Ant Leader has many skills, they recognize that they are stronger with their team.	The Spider Leader is an expert in forward planning and playing the game on their own territory.	The Fly Leader recognizes that the job is not always glamorous but persistence is important to attain goals.

After the brainstorming has been done and the connections have been made, it may be that the different leadership styles can be compared and one is obviously better than the others. Some may even be lessons in what not to do. Or, as in the above example, it may be that lessons can be learned from every style, so that (for example) every leader should have a bit of ant, spider, and fly in them! The important thing is that this is a fresh (and fun) way to approach an issue or idea.

Exercise 13
Stimulus – What Do You See?

The final exercise with random objects is a stimulus exercise and can be used just as a creative warm-up or it can then be connected to the project or idea you are working on. This exercise works by picking something random – it could be some shapes or a picture of part of an object that is not necessarily obvious – and asking what you can see? It is a variant on the famous *Rorschach Test* which asks participants what they see when they look at a randomly created inkblot. The second part is to ask how what you see could be connected to your project or idea.

Examples of stimuli for "What Do You See?":

The answers can, of course, start off literally (a triangle in front of a circle, tree branches, the sea) but the idea is then to get more abstract and take it further (e.g. the setting sun behind a mountain, a network of connections, a man jogging). As with all exercises, the more ideas you can create the better, as this will give you more to work with. This exercise also benefits from remembering the lessons of considering different perspectives in Chapter 7. For example, if you turn the first picture above on its side, it could be a *Pac-Man* eating or shouting.

2) The comparison

There are some similarities between this type of connection and the random objects in section 1) above, especially because you can use a random object or idea for the comparison. However, this type of exercise is designed to dig deeper into the two things being examined and find meaningful comparisons between them. This works particularly well when the things being compared have at least certain similarities e.g. comparing two jobs, two ideas, or two places.

Comparing is a natural skill that we do all the time. We are taught it at school but we also look around and constantly compare ourselves and our situations to others. In part, this is because humans are societal creatures and we need to see how we are doing relative to other people in order to ensure that we fit into society.

As an Englishman living in America, I find myself constantly comparing the two countries to try to make sense of the situations I find myself in and also to help create and appreciate new ideas. The language is so similar, yet so critically different at important points. Every British person knows that Americans walk on the "sidewalk." In the UK it is called the "pavement." What most British people don't know is that in America, the "pavement" is the road surface. Imagine the danger when I first came to America if I told my kids to walk on the pavement! After many years of comparing the two countries, I now have enough ideas to create a fantastic new country (e.g. Briterica? Ameritain?). If only I could find an available island somewhere in the mid-Atlantic!

Exercise 14
Analogy

This exercise works by comparing two different things that nevertheless share a category (e.g. an object, job or idea). It will be easier to make comparisons the less abstract or random the two categories are. Imagine you wanted to improve your work team. You could do an analogy exercise by comparing it to a soccer team. The next step is to list as many things as you can related to each team.

Work team	Soccer team
• 8 members	• 11 players
• 1 boss	• 1 captain
• Boss tells team members what to do	• Uniform
• Team members stay in the same role	• Clear goal (to score a goal and not concede any)
• Work in cubicles	• Outside or inside
• Team meeting (once a week)	• Crowd/supporters
• Produce report after 1 month	• Regularly meets other teams
• Different backgrounds/ expertise	• Plays 90 minutes
• Communicate mostly by email	• Individuals in different positions
• Not everyone sees all other team members each day	• 15-minute break at half-time
• Gives presentations to CEO	• Attack/defense
	• Practice skills
	• Penalties

Having got some thoughts down, the next stage is to look for similarities and differences and to categorize them. The final step is to look at what ideas might flow from the comparison. For example, a few could be:

Category	Work team	Soccer team	Ideas
Location	• Work in cubicles	• Outside or inside • Travel to away games	• Freshen the team by working in different locations? • Go outside together?
Time together	• Team meeting (once a week) • Not everyone sees all other team members each day	• Plays 90 minutes together	• Meet more often (every day)? • Motivate each other before starting work each day? • Come together at end of day to give feedback and support each other?
Identity/ Labeling	• Finance Department	• Uniform	• Wear something or give the team something so they can be proud of their department e.g. pin, t-shirt?
Who sees the work	• Team presents to CEO	• Crowd/ fans	• Find a way to feed the group's work to a bigger audience?

Exercise 15

Idea Box

The Idea Box is a technique to generate new ideas by modifying the variables of an idea or creation. Author Michael Michalko describes how this technique was even used by the great artist and inventor Leonardo da Vinci to randomly change the facial features of his sketches and caricatures.[71]

Start by deciding what it is that you want to create or what problem you would like to solve. Then list a number of important variables. For example, if you were writing a novel, your variables might be: Character, Setting, Theme, and Problem. You could choose more variables if you wished. Next, you list as many different possibilities as you can think of for each variable. Finally, go randomly through the box picking one possibility from each variable. Then look at that collection of variables as a whole and compare it to other random collections of variables.

An advantage of this exercise is the number of possible combinations of ideas you can make. For example, the box on the following page, which shows some simple ideas for writing a novel, has 625 different possible connections. It would be easy to come up with many more possible answers. You do not need to limit yourself to just five answers per variable!

From the ideas circled in this box, you can see the idea sketched out for an idea of a novel like George Orwell's *Animal Farm*.

	PLOT FOR A NOVEL			
	Characters	Setting	Theme	Problem
1	Prince	Castle	Adventure	Need to find treasure
2	Teacher	(Farm)	Love	Being lost
3	Orphan	Tropical Island	War	(Fight for freedom)
4	Dog	Forest	(Dictatorship)	Stranger in a foreign land
5	(Pig)	City	Friendship	Going mad

3) The path

Have you ever met anyone in life who sailed smoothly along their path, from A to B to C to D without storms or getting blown off course along the way? It seems unlikely because most people's lives are not predictable. At age 13, when I set my heart on becoming an English criminal barrister (a lawyer who wears a funny wig in court), I never imagined that one day I would be standing in an American classroom explaining to a class of 7-year olds how America won independence from Britain!

What are the lessons from this?

- You cannot always know what to expect in life.

- Life is not just a single path but a network of rich and diverse possibilities.

- Even if you cannot control every step, the more alert and open to the possibilities you are, the more you will see and the greater control you can have over them.

After several warnings in this book about the dangers of incremental growth, this set of exercises is perhaps most akin to incremental growth, in that the starting point is where you are now. The exercises have considerable value though because they require exploration of the possibilities of different ideas that will guide your way along the path you want to travel, whether that path is a life goal, a creative project, or an idea. These types of exercises might also be easier for those who struggle at first with more abstract thinking.

Exercise 16
Lotus Blossom

The Lotus Blossom is an exercise from Japan where you start with a central idea or problem and then work out (ideally) eight main themes or issues connected to the original idea or problem. The central idea is written in the middle of a sheet of paper and the eight main issues are written around the outside. Next, each of the eight main issues is considered as a central theme and eight further issues are identified and written around each one.

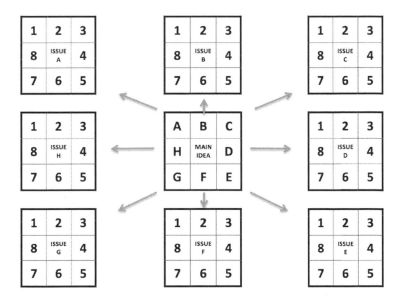

The process is akin to peeling back the issues one by one just as one might peel the petals of a flower. At the end, if fully completed, there will be 64 sub-issues to consider. The value as you go through this is that you see how the main idea evolves and how sub-issues might be connected to each other and new themes and patterns emerge.

Exercise 17
Fishbone Analysis

This is another exercise from Japan that is particularly helpful for looking at cause and effect. An issue, idea or problem for analysis is written in the fish's head. A number of major causes of the problem or important parts of the idea are then identified and written on the outer edges of the fishbone diagram. Next to each cause, a number of relevant factors for consideration are then listed.

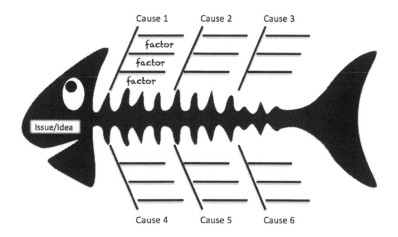

The purpose of this analysis is to better understand the issue rather than to solve the problem, but naturally, any solution is likely to be clearer once the potential cause or causes have been identified. If this is used for creative ideas, then the fish bones can be key components of the idea or different directions to explore. It could even be combined with some of the different perspective ideas in Chapter 7 to list the different ways an idea can be considered.

Exercise 18
Story Trail

The Story Trail is a nice exercise just to stimulate creativity by itself or it can be used to generate connections to an existing idea or issue. In its simplest form, go for a walk and identify five objects. You can collect them (if allowed), photograph them, note them or just remember them. One of the benefits of this is that walking is a relaxing activity, a mental break, physical exercise, and often the perfect situation to find a creative stimulus.

When you get back, the challenge is to write or tell a story incorporating the objects found. The objects should connect to each other in the story in the same order in which they were found. There will be other obvious and less obvious connections between the objects, probably depending on how close together you found the objects and how random you were in your selection!

If you wanted to work on an idea or problem, you could do exactly the same exercise, but this time that idea or problem will be the starting point of the story and you then have to relate the objects you found to the idea or problem in the story. In other words, you could do Exercise 11 (Perfectly Random) for each object you found.

Creative Strength:
Making Connections – Summary

Random objects

- Perfectly Random
- If We Were All Bugs (Connecting To Categories)
- Stimulus – What Do You See?

The comparison

- Analogy
- Idea Box

The path

- Lotus Blossom
- Fishbone Analysis
- Story Trail

Chapter 9

Creative Strength: Be A Child

There is an inherent tragedy in growing up. Toddlers and children start out life as fantastically inquisitive and creative beings whose brains are constantly developing as we saw in Chapter 1. But by adulthood, much of that creativity seems to have disappeared, or worse, been beaten out of them. I believe that these changes are partly natural as we have seen that the adult brain does not change as much as a young brain. On the other hand, I believe another large factor is the obsessive focus society places on having "good" exam results, a college education, jobs, and money, all of which seem to require conforming and following what other people do.

One day, when my son Jonathan was 4, I was looking around a preschool. The preschool teacher was nice and eager to please. She enthusiastically told me, "If you send Jonathan to this school, we can get him ready for kindergarten. You don't want him going there next year unprepared!" As well meaning as the comment was, isn't it astonishing? The implication was that already he would be behind if he was not being educated at age 4!

Once our children get to school, the focus quickly moves on to standardized testing and preparing every student for college. When our 5-year-olds start kindergarten, they only have 13 years left before college so clearly, there's no time to lose! In spite of the OECD survey (mentioned in Chapter 3) which reports that many countries' curriculums consider creativity to be a 21st-century skill, in reality, it often seems that very little focus at school is given to creativity and play. By the time our schools and colleges have taken our creative toddlers and worked on them for 20 years, there is a real danger that they are spat out as a colony of cloned ants (again, see Chapter 3). Or as educator Neil Postman put it, **"children enter school as question marks and come out as periods."**[72] Then, when it is too late, we worry that they don't have the creative skills our society and organizations need to survive!

If we want to be creative, it makes a great deal of sense to emulate children - those masters of creativity! In this chapter we will examine three types of creativity that come naturally to children:

- **Play**
- **Fun Challenges**
- **Imagination**

1) Play

The ability to play is one of the characteristics that set humans apart from most animals, guiding us toward creativity and the unique path we have been traveling for so long now. A sad trend in schools is the decline in recess time[73] yet the situation is even worse in offices. **Almost no adults get recess time when they are at work!**

We often don't value play and creativity like we should. I know I'm not perfect either. I'll never forget when Jonathan had show and tell at his first pre-school when he was just 3 years old. He had to choose a toy to bring in – just one – from the millions he already seemed to have acquired. After careful consideration, he was insistent on taking in "Snakey" which happened to be an old, screwed-up shopping receipt. I tried to dissuade him but he was insistent so Snakey went into school. What happened next was shocking. Because I was embarrassed, I explained to his teacher that we did have "real" toys at home. **I feared her judgment more than I valued my son's creativity!** I later realized my mistake and it was a good lesson to learn.

Perhaps the final thought about the importance of play should be an old and famous quote that, over the years, has been attributed to a few different people:[74]

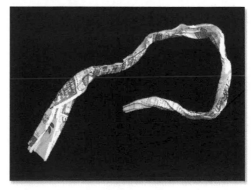

"**We don't stop playing because we grow old. We grow old because we stop playing.**"

Exercise 19
Free Play

Free play means exactly what it sounds like. It means playing for the sake of playing. There does not need to be a particular objective in mind. It does not matter what or who you play with. There are many well-documented benefits to play such as helping to develop learning and creative problem solving.[75]

You can, of course, play with items that are relevant to a particular problem or invention or idea and you may find a new solution with them. Or else, the mere act of playing can put you in a different mindset, ready to be more creative.

In schools and offices, people have often been told off or criticized for playing or fidgeting rather than "concentrating" on the task at hand. When I was teacher training with a group of adults in England, every science class had a variety of materials placed in the middle of our tables at the beginning of the lesson. It amused me that even though we were all adults who would soon be teachers, we could not stop ourselves from playing with all of the materials before we were supposed to. We were no better than any class of young children I ever taught!

As the value and benefits of play have been slowly realized over the years, office and desktop toys have become all the rage. In Appendix 3, I list some basic items you could have at home and in the office to allow simple play wherever you are.

Exercise 20
Art & Doodling

Art seems to intimidate many people yet it is something all children start out doing enthusiastically. Picasso said, **"Every child is an artist. The problem is how to remain an artist when you grow up."** You can see what he means. He recognized we are all creative but that in the adult world there are obstacles that get in the way of our creativity. Art is highly subjective so almost anything can count as art if you wish. At one end of the artistic spectrum, if you learned a new skill such as painting fine art portraits or photography, that would undoubtedly help your brain forge new connections (see Chapter 2). Alternatively, at the other end of the spectrum, there is great value in merely making marks. After all, this is what our ancestors started doing in caves 40,000 years ago and we have been making marks ever since. The children's book *The Dot* by Peter Reynolds wonderfully highlights the significance of making even a simple dot on paper.[76] Here are four fun artistic exercises:

Make modern art like Kandinsky

Wassily Kandinsky was a Russian abstract painter who specialized in paintings using bold, bright blocks of color and lines. Start drawing shapes and lines on a sheet of paper and color some in. Pastels and charcoal work very well for this. Every so often, turn the page

around and work elsewhere. This exercise works particularly well with small groups where one person finishes what another started. When most of the page is filled in, stand back and admire your work. It is amazing how authentic it will look.

Disruption

This is a clever exercise shown to me by artist Fred Mandell.[77] Draw some shapes on paper. Cut them out and stick them down onto a different colored piece of paper. Then cut that colored paper in half. You may initially feel reluctant to spoil your creation by cutting it in half. That is exactly the point! The act of cutting dramatically changes the nature of what you have produced as well as forcing you to give up any attachment you had to the first object. Repeat the process of creating new shapes, adding them to the colored paper but then cutting up that paper. The disruption that occurs prevents you from falling in love with any one idea and forces you to keep seeing new possibilities, which is a very creative experience.

Visualize like da Vinci

Leonardo da Vinci would relax, close his eyes and then cover a sheet of paper with lines and scribbles.[78] Draw what you want to and how you want to. You could do this with a particular challenge in mind or just do it and see where it takes you. When finished, examine the drawing and see what you notice. What patterns are there? What does it make you think of? What ideas does that lead to?

Doodle

Probably everyone has doodled in their life and there are many famous examples to see.[79] In her book, *The Doodle Revolution*,[80] Sunni Brown champions the cause of doodling claiming that it is really thinking in disguise. Doodling naturally encompasses different learning styles (visual, auditory, kinesthetic) and can increase creativity and memory. Doodles can vary from being on a small sheet of paper or in a book to big "Infodoodles" produced by groups at work who might be doing some strategic planning. As with the previous exercise, choose whether to doodle randomly and see where it takes you or be more purposeful and represent ideas connected to your purpose.

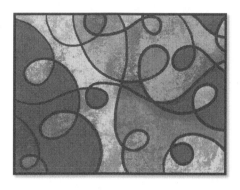

Exercise 21
Improvisation

"Improv" has become particularly popular in comedy circles and increasingly adults are trying it as they recognize benefits it can bring. An improv situation typically involves quick thinking, going with the flow, making mistakes and working with others. It is a refreshing change from a world where there is usually great importance put on being well prepared, uncontroversial and not making mistakes.

Improvisation is something that children do very naturally, but adults usually need a little help and guidance to do. For example, one golden rule of improv is to work with the situation/dialogue that you are given rather than to dispute it.

There are lots of ways to bring improv into your life:

- Do something new.

- Go somewhere different.

- Engage with new people.

You can play specific improv games too:

- **Storytelling (1)** – each person tells one line of a story and the next person must continue it.

- **Storytelling (2)** – write out some words on paper and place them face down. Tell a story and at key points pick up a piece of paper, read the word out, and continue the story.

- **Proverb Game** – Each person adds one word to a sentence to make a wise saying. The key is not to think too much but say what comes into your head and seems to fit. E.g. "The ... sun ... is ... often ... not ... that ... visible."

- **Table Topics** – a favorite public speaking exercise at Toastmasters meetings[81] is where participants have to give a 1-2 minute impromptu speech about a question they have only just heard. After a brief pause for thought, the speeches often start as a bit of a stream of consciousness, but practice makes them much easier to do!

2) Fun challenges

The psychologist Maslow said, **"almost all creativity involves purposeful play"** and it is certainly possible to play with a lot more focus and purpose than mere free play. When it comes to purposeful games and crafts, there is no one more focused than my daughter Jasmine. I'm always being asked for paper, scissors, tape, glue, staples and so on. Once she has an idea about making something in her head, she single-mindedly pursues it, regardless of whether it's time for bed, school or anything else!

At home recently I found a whole bunch of screwed up pieces of paper on my windowsill with faces on. Jasmine told me they were monster eggs. My initial concern at the mess was quickly displaced when she said: "Yes I can make anything I want. Daddy – I've decided you never need to go to the toy store again!"

It should be noted that at this point, Jonathan poked his head up from the computer game he was playing, to explain that we may still need to visit toy shops for him. But Jasmine countered with: "Why? Nobody needs them when you can make toys!"

Fun challenges have often been the preserve of team-building exercises on staff away days but there is no reason why they should not be more commonly used. Another trend that is increasing in popularity is gamification. This is where tasks are adapted to include game-like elements and rules (e.g. point scoring, competition with others) to encourage participation and output in the task at hand. One example is the invention of *Wii Fit* by Shigeru Miyamoto which came about through his desire to gamify losing weight and to make it fun.

The following exercises can be used for specific purposes or more generally for fun, teambuilding and to get into a creative mindset.

Exercise 22
Specific Purpose Challenge

This is a classic type of challenge of which there are numerous variants. Basically, it is comprised of two parts: (1) Here is the specific challenge, and (2) these are the tools available.

Within that framework, you could create just about any challenge you want to. Some well-known examples are:

- *Marshmallow Challenge:*[82] How tall a structure can you build in 18 minutes using spaghetti, tape, string and a marshmallow?

- How far can you make a paper airplane fly?

- How strong a bridge can you make using paper (and/or other materials)?

- Can you build a structure to safely capture an egg dropped from a height?

Note: When done in teams, you can often notice a lot about people and the way they work. Diverse teams usually work much better. It is also interesting to have another go at the challenge after people have seen what others have done and what was successful. This is not cheating as they may well then incorporate their own improvements to an idea.

Exercise 23
Cardboard Boxes

Cardboard boxes are everywhere and it would be strange to write a book about creativity without acknowledging the amazing power of the simple cardboard box.

Everyone knows that a child typically prefers the cardboard box to the expensive toy that came inside. It's obvious why. The toy has one function but the cardboard box is an endless world of imagination and adventure. I'm not a huge fan of the phrase, "think outside the box" because it is often used as a cliché when people want to pretend that they are being creative. Saying that phrase alone does not make something creative! The funny thing is that while we're always told to "think outside the box" **children do their thinking *inside* the box**!

The cardboard box is so amazing that in 2005, it was inducted into The Strong National Museum of Play's National Toy Hall of Fame.[83] In 2011, 9-year-old Caine Monroy built an arcade out of boxes in his Dad's used auto parts store in Los Angeles. An emotional video (which you should watch if you've never seen it)[84] went viral and his creation became world famous. Now there is a *Global Cardboard Challenge* where kids are encouraged "to build anything they can dream up using cardboard, recycled materials, and imagination."[85]

Cardboard box exercises:

- Do the *Global Cardboard Challenge*.

- Use the cardboard box as the material for a Specific Purpose Challenge.

- Pretend to be different people and think how they would use the box.

- Tell a story using the box as a prop in as many different ways as possible.

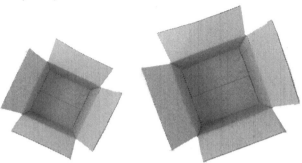

Exercise 24
Ultimate Challenge

The Ultimate Challenge differs from those above in that it poses a much bigger challenge and the participants are not expected to build something that will actually solve the challenge in reality. Instead, they will come up with ideas to solve the challenge. If materials are available then they can build a prototype invention. I once taught a boy who was habitually late for school. He "invented" a machine that would wake him up and get him to school on time every day!

This is a good exercise for brainstorming anything from the world's biggest problems to personal or corporate goals:

- How can we end pollution?

- What can we do about sea levels rising?

- How can we end hunger?

- How can our company become number 1?

- How can I double my sales?

- How can I get fit?

Remember, as with all creative exercises, the exercise itself may not necessarily produce an answer that can be implemented, but **the process of being creative is likely to open you up to possibilities that you were not aware of.**

Exercise 25
"But Wait – There's More!"
(The Commercial)

This is a fun activity that can build on Exercise 24 (Ultimate Challenge) and can also work as Exercise 21 (Improvisation). The task is to take an idea, invention or solution and give a commercial or presentation to others, explaining why such idea or invention is exactly what they need. Of course, people do this in real life, but the idea in this context is again to have fun while stretching the bounds of plausibility.

Good topics include:

• An invention to sell snow to Eskimos.

• The clothing of the future.

• A way to revolutionize work/exercise/travel etc.

• The most delicious new food/drink.

This exercise can be performed in competition with others. Another version of it is the Balloon Debate. Each person in a group takes on the role of a different character in a hot air balloon that is sinking and some must be cast overboard to lighten the load. The characters must debate why they are more important or valuable than the others and therefore why they should stay in the balloon.

3) Imagination

As a teacher, I once asked my 2nd Grade class for ideas when I was planning a class reward. One girl raised her hand: "Mr. Pink, can we go to Italy?"

I was about to dismiss the idea out of hand when it occurred to me that maybe there was a way. What if we could bring Italy into our classroom? A few days later, we had an Italian afternoon where we made pizza, learned Italian and sang Italian opera songs.

There were two valuable lessons from this experience. First, children's imagination knows no bounds. It is endlessly ambitious. Second, **when you start to think about things and use your imagination, there is often a way of making things work**.

Imagination is always going to be an important tool when it comes to exercising creativity. We saw in Chapter 2, how imagination was able to help achieve physical accomplishments such as playing the piano or exercising. All of us imagine, but often we feel guilty for wasting time rather than enjoying the moment or seeing how it could be helpful to us. Einstein said, **"Imagination is more important than knowledge,"**[86] and credited his discovery of the General Theory of Relativity in part to imagining chasing a beam of light.[87]

Another reason why imagination is so important is given by Doug Hall: **"New product ideas that anticipate the future are 10 times more predictive of success than those that simply listen to the voice of the customer."**[88] An obvious example of this is Apple who would no doubt claim to know what we need before we know ourselves!

Exercise 26
What If?

There is a strong case for saying that **the two most important words in the English language are *"what if?"*** Without these two tiny words, our world would not exist. Every great question that advanced civilization started with "what if?" For example:

- **What if** we could fly?

- **What if** we could speak to someone on the other side of the world?

- **What if** we could walk on the moon?

Imagine if you traveled back in time 200 years and told the people living then that you had a small machine that:

- Could let you take pictures or record a living event

- Could let you play millions of songs

- Could let you speak to someone on the other side of the world

- Could let you see someone moving in real time on the other side of the world

- Allowed you to look up any piece of information you wanted

The people then would think you were crazy or maybe a witch! Yet now we take all of these advances (that started with a "what if?") for granted.

As with many creative exercises, you can let this exercise take you where you want (e.g. starting with a daydream) or you can think of a specific problem or challenge and start to frame "what if?" questions connected to it.

- What if I didn't have to work?

- What if I could go anywhere I wanted?

- What if I was the richest person on earth?

- What if I took up a new hobby?

- What if we got rid of elections?

Then try to answer the question, drawing out as much detail as you can. Part of the essence of the imagination skill is visualization and the more clearly you can imagine things, the easier the process becomes. As you answer a "what if?" question, you are likely to create further such questions, creating an even more detailed picture.

Exercise 27
Kids' World

Researchers Darya Zabelina and Michael Robinson, of North Dakota State University, wanted to test the theory that thinking like children enhanced the creativity of adults. They asked two groups of students to write about what they would do if they had a day off from school. One group wrote as their present day selves and the second group as their 7-year-old selves. The second group produced more interesting results and subsequently performed with more originality on a creativity test. Thinking like a child really does help creativity![89]

All children know that anything is possible if we use our imagination more. This exercise asks you to be as childlike as possible in creating an imaginary world or a different world to the world you inhabit. It could be just for fun or it could be related to a challenge or future goal.

Think about what you can see, smell, hear, taste and touch. Role-playing and investigating an imaginary or historical world is a major technique used in teaching children in schools, as well as engaging visitors in museums. If it helps, you can start by creating or having a stimulus which might be a real object, or by researching an area of the world you want to visit. *Google Maps* and *Street View* allow you to go just about anywhere in the world now!

In getting into the child's mindset, it might help to remember some of their qualities. You do not have to do all of these, but some may help you use your imagination:

- There are **no rules** limiting your imagination.

- **Anything is possible.** Children love absurdity (and superpowers).

- **Everyone is a friend** (unless they are an enemy!).

- **Immerse yourself** in your world (but watch out for dinosaurs and pirates).

- **Be impulsive, spontaneous** and **go with the flow**. Children often don't stop to think.

- **Follow your instinct.**

- **Have fun.** Laugh.

- **Treat every day as a new day full of possibility.** As an adult, every day is loaded with the implications of previous days and events. For a child, every day is a blank slate of opportunity.

- **Be messy**! Kids don't worry about how they look or tidiness. Mud, paint, chalk and sand are creative tools not dangerous, messy substances.

- **Play, Play, Play**!

Exercise 28
Dream or Daydream

The first two exercises based on imagination involved either a specific question ("what if?") or creating a specific imaginary world. The final exercise involves neither. Allow ideas and creativity to come to you either by daydreaming (if you are awake) or dreaming (if you are asleep!). Unlike the other exercises, there is no need for a particular stimulus or input. Let your mind wander and see where it takes you.

Author Neil Gaiman recommends being bored (which really means switching off from the constant distractions that occupy every moment of our lives – phones, emails, and so on) so that we can pay attention to our creativity:

"You get ideas from daydreaming. You get ideas from being bored. You get ideas all the time."[90]

Everyone has a "sleep cycle" of sleep and dreams and waking each night. The average sleep cycle is about 90 minutes. Typically a dream occurs toward the end of the cycle. Most people are not aware of waking before they enter their next sleep cycle. You can keep a sleep journal to record when you go to sleep and wake up (uninterrupted) and find out how long your cycle is.[91] Waking up before a cycle finishes is one reason you can feel really tired when you wake up. Setting an alarm slightly before a sleep cycle finishes though can also be a way of interrupting a dream so you can record what is happening.

Whether dreaming or daydreaming, one important thing to consider is how you will capture the ideas that come from them. It is well known that dreams are quickly forgotten so one idea is to keep a notebook or recorder by the bed so you can record ideas as soon as you awake. Throughout the day, you can also keep notebooks on you or use a phone to record ideas. From now on, whenever you have to wait for something, you have been presented with an opportunity for creativity!

Creative Strength:
Be A Child – Summary

Play

- Free Play
- Art & Doodling
- Improvisation

Fun Challenges

- Specific Purpose Challenge
- Cardboard Boxes
- The Ultimate Challenge
- "But Wait – There's More!" (The Commercial)

Imagination

- What If?
- Kids' World
- Dream or Daydream

Chapter 10

Creative Stamina: Finding Sustainable Ideas

My son Jonathan is now 9. He and I enjoy playing soccer together. Yet I have many advantages over him. I'm bigger. I'm faster. I'm stronger. So who wins our games? He does! The problem is that after 10 minutes I'm exhausted. He could keep playing all day. He has greater stamina than I do.

In creativity, stamina is really important too. The last three chapters (Creative Strength) have all focused on generating ideas. But generating ideas alone is not enough for creativity. Remember the definition of creativity:

Creativity is an **original idea** that has **value.**

Eventually, the ideas have to be evaluated to consider whether they are original and have value. In other words, can the idea keep running or will it inevitably die? I call this stage Creative Stamina.

When exercising Creative Strength, for the most part, it makes sense to avoid the judgment that comes with Creative Stamina. Such judgment can restrict your creative freedom. However, during the Creative Stamina stage, it may be after a period of evaluating and judging ideas that you need to return to the Creative Strength stage to generate further ideas as you refine and develop your idea.

In some ways, this whole process is reminiscent of the way we saw our brains work in Chapters 1 and 2. When we do new things, the synapses in our brains make new connections just as much Creative Strength involves making new connections. But what our brain doesn't need, it gets rid of by pruning the synapses so that it remains efficient. After we have generated many ideas, Creative Stamina requires us to get rid of the ones that don't work and focus on those that will.

1) Creative Stamina requires a shift in attitude

As noted above, it is important to recognize that Creative Stamina requires a different mindset to the Creative Strength stage. **BUT**, it is still important to remain positive and not disparage the Creative Strength process. Reasons for this include:

- You may need to go back to the Creative Strength stage.

- There may be some overlap between the Creative Strength and Creative Stamina stages.

- You (or the people around you) will be in the Creative Strength stage in the future and you don't want actions and attitudes in the current Creative Stamina stage to inhibit future creativity.

- Why not be nice and positive rather than nasty and negative?!

Here are three key attitudes for the Creative Stamina stage:

A) Stay positive, not negative

What you say can have a big influence on an outcome. Instead of saying, "Yes, but …" try saying, "Yes, and …" This allows you to focus on the good aspects of an idea rather than dismissing an idea too quickly. Creativity expert Paul Sloane gives a similar magic sentence:[92]

"That sounds interesting. How can we make it work?"

Such a sentence allows the atmosphere of welcoming creativity and open-mindedness to be maintained, even though you are judging and evaluating an idea.

B) Keep the novelty alive

Now that the serious work of evaluating an idea is upon you, it is important not to run for safety by choosing the least risky ideas. As discussed in Chapter 3, one of the reasons creativity is so important is the need to move away from continuous improvement toward discontinuous innovation. That will not happen if you disregard your more original or unusual ideas and always choose your safest ideas.

Keeping the novelty alive also recognizes that new possibilities may open themselves up. There are numerous accidental inventions (microwaves, *Post-It Notes*, *Play-Doh* to name a few) that all started out for different reasons from those that they subsequently became famous for.

C) Be persistent

Creative Stamina can be a harder step than Creative Strength. Some people prefer starting projects to finishing them. There can be lots of fun in the initial stages of creating ideas and that fun can disappear when the reality hits of having to make something work. Stick with it! Remember Dyson's 5,126 failures before getting his bagless vacuum cleaner right.

Here is a list of useful questions to help you keep working through the Creative Stamina stage:

- What is your goal?

- What 3 steps can you do to make this work?

- How can you build on the strengths?

- How can you overcome weaknesses?

- Who can help you?

- Where can you get advice and support from?

- How can you test the idea?

- How can you overcome fear?

- How can you make your idea more appealing to other people?

- What other possibilities might there be?

2) Creative Stamina exercises

When you have completed your Creative Strength exercises and you have a number of ideas, you can then use the Creative Stamina exercises to help choose what you wish to focus on. For the purposes of the exercises on the following pages, I will assume that a group of people is evaluating the ideas. It is certainly possible to use the exercises by yourself, but it would often be helpful to have the input of different people.

Exercise 29
Voting

There are many different ways that voting can work as a way to choose which ideas to focus on. If there are many ideas and many people, one method is to use dot voting. Write or display all the ideas being considered on a wall. Each person gets (for example) five votes and can place a dot (representing one vote) against each idea that they like. It will quickly become evident which ideas are the most popular. If a person feels particularly strongly about a certain idea then they can award more than one vote to it.

Warning: Initially, you want to avoid people voting according to how others are voting, so you may want people to think about the options first before going to place their votes.

A variation of this is called Blue-Sky Voting by Professor Gerard Puccio.[93] Each person is given a number of green and blue votes. Green represents ideas that are straightforward and easy to implement. You can proceed with them immediately. The blue votes represent the more original (and creative) ideas but are not necessarily easy to implement straight away. Nevertheless, you are excited about these ideas and will be thinking about a way to make them work in the future.

These blue votes are similar to the yellow ideas in the next exercise.

Exercise 30
HOW WOW NOW Box

This exercise is a matrix-based exercise usually called the COCD Box (inspired by Mark Raison and developed by the Center for Development of Creative Thinking). A grid is created focusing on two different factors: (1) How feasible an idea is (or how easy it is to implement) and (2) how original an idea is. The box creates three categories of ideas that are valuable. Blue and red ideas can be implemented immediately. Red ideas are the truly creative ones. Although yellow ideas cannot yet be implemented, they are ideas to work toward in the future.

If a group is evaluating a large number of ideas, each member can be given a certain number of blue, red and yellow votes (which could be stickers). They place these next to the ideas accordingly. The ideas that are the most popular are then placed in the appropriate category according to whether they got mostly red, blue or yellow votes. When this initial stage is complete, the group can then discuss if they agree with the placement or whether certain ideas need to be moved.

Not (yet) feasible ideas	Do not pursue!	**YELLOW IDEAS** • Ideas for the future • Dreams and challenges • Stimulation for the brain • Can be the red ideas of tomorrow **HOW?**
Feasible ideas	**BLUE IDEAS** • Easy to implement • Few risks involved • High acceptability • Past examples available **NOW**	**RED IDEAS** • Innovative ideas • Breakthrough • Exciting ideas • Can be implemented **WOW!**
	Common ideas	**Original Ideas**

Exercise 31
$100 Test

This exercise is another way of showing what is most important to you. There is nothing like spending your own money to focus your attention, rather than just voting for an idea. Imagine you are on *Shark Tank* (or *Dragon's Den* in the UK) and have $100 of your own money to allocate between your ideas. How would you divide the money up?

The exercise could work both by allocating money between different ideas or between different priorities connected to the same idea. Remember that the money represents hypothetical investment and should not be confused with the actual cost of doing something. As an investment, you should be looking for a return on your money so make sure you focus on what you think will give you the best return. An example is given on the next page.

$100 Test: Ways to make our team win the league		
Idea	**Cost**	**Why?**
New players	$20	New players are always useful, but we already have some good players.
New coach	$5	Our current coach is excellent.
Train harder	$15	Our team already trains harder than most.
Get new training equipment	$35	Our equipment is mostly outdated and breaking down.
Learn new strategies	$25	We're becoming predictable.
Sue the league for unfair rulings against us	$0	We never win in court and it's expensive.

Exercise 32
Start Stop Continue
Test

This is a simple exercise to evaluate different ideas or courses of action. It could also be used as a Creative Strength exercise to brainstorm new ideas rather than just a Creative Stamina exercise to evaluate ideas.

Ask the following questions:

- **Start**: What should we start doing that we have not been doing before? Why will this make a difference?

- **Stop**: What should we stop doing? What is a waste of our time? What is not helping us achieve our goals or pursue our mission?

- **Continue**: What are we already doing that is beneficial and working well? Can we improve this or leverage the results from it?

If this exercise is done in a group then each individual will contribute their thoughts and the group will discuss as a consensus as to what should be started, stopped or continued.

Start	Stop	Continue
Waking up at 6 am every day.	Checking emails throughout the day.	Taking short walks each day.
Making a to-do list with prioritized tasks before going to bed.	Reacting to small tasks and distractions that are not aligned to prioritized tasks.	Exercising daily.

Exercise 33
NUF (New Useful Feasible) Test

The NUF test assesses similar criteria to the HOW WOW NOW Box but in a slightly different way. Ideas are scored according to how new, useful and feasible they are (out of 10 possible points):

- **New**: How original is the idea? (Remember creativity requires originality!) Has it been done before?

- **Useful**: Does it do what it is supposed to? Does it solve a problem? Does it avoid creating new problems?

- **Feasible**: Can it be implemented? Is the cost prohibitive? Who will need to be persuaded?

Idea	New	Useful	Feasible	Total
Flying car	10	10	1	21
Windowless car	8	1	10	19
Driverless car	8	10	7	25
Passenger-less car	9	3	10	22

You can also write comments next to the ideas. If done in a group, scoring can be the total or an average of people's scores. After the initial scoring is complete, the numbers can still be discussed to see if they make sense or should be adjusted.

Creative Stamina:
Finding Sustainable Ideas – Summary

Attitudes

- Stay positive, not negative
- Keep the novelty alive
- Be persistent

Exercises

- Voting
- HOW WOW NOW Box
- $100 Test
- Start Stop Continue Test
- NUF Test

Part 4

The Creative Juice Bar

Well done! You've had a good work out. Now let's sit in the Creative Juice Bar and have a chat about what happens next.

Chapter 11

How To Be Creative In Any Situation

By focusing on different themes in creativity, one of my purposes of writing this book is to show you how you can be creative in any situation. In the past, whenever the clarion call for creativity sounded, the typical response was to have a "brainstorming" session. The success of such a session would depend on numerous factors such as how healthy the creative environment was (see Chapters 5 and 6). Sometimes, a trainer might know a specific creative exercise and get the people to perform it. But by treating all exercises the same and by failing to acknowledge the two stages of the creative process, there was always a risk that such exercises would be ineffective.

The two stages of the creative process are Creative Strength and Creative Stamina. Together, we might visualize them like the diagram on the following page:

Two Stages of the Creative Process

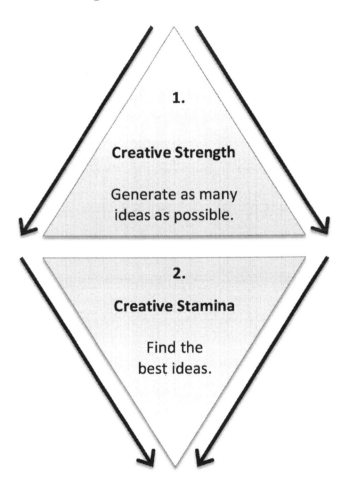

On the next page, I have created a simple flowchart of questions to ask yourself in any creative situation. These questions relate to the chapters in this book, which you can refer back to. By following these questions, you should be able to be creative in any situation.

How To Be Creative In Any Situation

Stage 1: Creative Strength

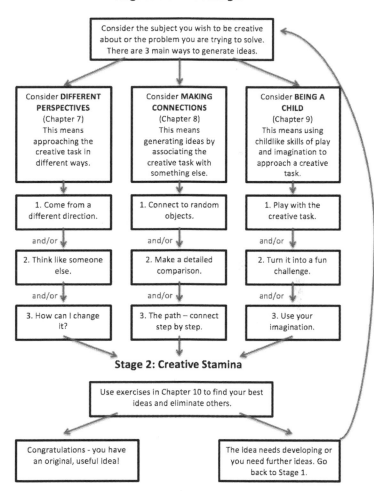

Consider the subject you wish to be creative about or the problem you are trying to solve. There are 3 main ways to generate ideas.

| Consider **DIFFERENT PERSPECTIVES** (Chapter 7) This means approaching the creative task in different ways. | Consider **MAKING CONNECTIONS** (Chapter 8) This means generating ideas by associating the creative task with something else. | Consider **BEING A CHILD** (Chapter 9) This means using childlike skills of play and imagination to approach a creative task. |

| 1. Come from a different direction. | 1. Connect to random objects. | 1. Play with the creative task. |

and/or

| 2. Think like someone else. | 2. Make a detailed comparison. | 2. Turn it into a fun challenge. |

and/or

| 3. How can I change it? | 3. The path – connect step by step. | 3. Use your imagination. |

Stage 2: Creative Stamina

Use exercises in Chapter 10 to find your best ideas and eliminate others.

Congratulations - you have an original, useful idea!

The idea needs developing or you need further ideas. Go back to Stage 1.

Chapter 12

The Thinking Revolution Revisited

I hope the journey through this book has left you with a much clearer picture of **how** to be creative and **why** to be creative. If we look again at the Declaration of Creativity, you can see it is possible to split it into sections.

Declaration of Creativity

The Facts	1. "Creativity" is not an elitist word.
	2. Everyone is creative.
The Need	3. Creativity is essential to a healthy, happy, purposeful life.
	4. Creativity is essential for future human success.
The Action	5. Creativity can be learned and should be exercised.
	6. Creativity should be encouraged and appreciated whenever possible.

The **facts** of creativity and the **need** for creativity have to be believed and then spread far and wide. But it is the **action** which will make a difference in your life and which can change the world. I hope you will join the Creativity Revolution and sign the Declaration of Creativity.

In the appendices you will find:

- Sample answers to the creative assessment questions in Chapter 4;

- Key quotes from this book;

- Suggestions about equipment you can use to make your own creative toolbox;

- Some sample Brainarium creative exercises and ways to connect with me; and

- References from throughout this book.

Never forget that you have a $100 million brain that is waiting to do something creative. Why not start right away? Good luck!

Appendix 1

Sample Answers To The Creative Assessment

The way this works

Please remember that there are no correct answers in creativity. Why then are there sample answers? The first reason is to help show examples of answers that are more or less creative and to explain why. The second reason is so that you can learn from them. Remember our fifth principle in the Declaration of Creativity is that creativity can be learned.

For example, suppose that you answered Question 1 and filled in all the boxes much like Answer A on the next page. It may never even have occurred to you to draw outside the box or link the boxes together. Don't worry! It doesn't mean you're not creative. Next time you see something like that, your brain will remember the creative possibility of drawing outside the box. That is how creativity is learned. It's not cheating!

Answers to the creative response questions

1. **Fill in the squares below with pictures or designs. Try to be as unusual as you can.**

Look at the two sample answers below:

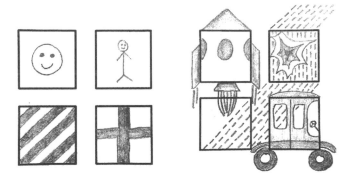

Answer A   **Answer B**

Answer A is a simple answer to the question. It also understood the question literally and drew in each box, but not outside. Answer B is a more creative answer for a number of reasons:

- The drawings are not limited to the boundaries of the squares but go outside them.

- Some of the squares have been transformed into different objects (e.g. a car, a rocket) rather than just a frame for a picture.

- Some of the squares are connected to each other suggesting the person saw them as part of a bigger picture rather than unrelated to each other.

- More detail is given in the drawing.

Note that this critique is not about the artistic ability of the answers. Answer B is more creative because it was less constrained by its interpretation of the question or by any assumed rules as to what was required.

2. In 1 minute, how many uses can you think of for a piece of chewing gum?

This is definitely a question where the more answers you can think of the better. The list of ideas is potentially never-ending. Remember Chapter 6 stresses the importance of going for quantity when coming up with ideas. Initial ideas are likely to be quite obvious:

- Food (though swallowing is not recommended!).
- Breath freshener.
- Teeth cleaner.
- Something to aid concentration.
- Trash.

Subsequent ideas might move further away from the obvious and start to incorporate ideas for which it was not primarily intended:

- Adhesive putty.
- A stress toy (if you have a big enough ball of it).
- Art (if stuck somewhere).

Eventually, with creative exercises and lateral thinking, you could end up with suggestions a long way from the obvious:

- A drug test (you chew it then submit it for testing).

- Draught excluder.

- Fishing bait.

- A weapon.

3. Describe what you see in the picture below:

This is another exercise where more answers are likely to lead to more creative ideas. Once again your answers might start more literally and gradually move toward less obvious ideas.

- Mixed shapes.

- A jack-in-the-box.

- Slam dunk!

- Firework display on a super blood moon night.

If you have finished reading the book then try applying the different creative techniques toward answering this question. For example, did you think to look at the picture from a different perspective?

This could now be a smiley face or a pirate with an eye-patch. From above, maybe it's a map of a river and buildings.

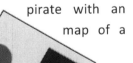

4. In what ways are nuts and books connected?

Making connections between different objects is one of the main creative themes and is covered in Chapter 8. More specifically, this question is an example of connecting random objects – Exercise 11 (Perfectly Random). This type of exercise invites you to look at the properties of the objects being compared to notice both similarities and differences.

- They both come from trees.

- They're both hard.

- They come in lots of different types.

- Some people love them. Others hate them (or are allergic to them)!

- Some people hoard books. Squirrels hoard nuts.

- They are good for you.

- You can write a book about nuts.

- You can be nuts about books.

5. Complete the picture below:

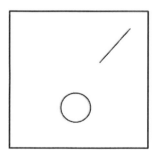

Look at the original picture and then look at the two sample answers on the following page:

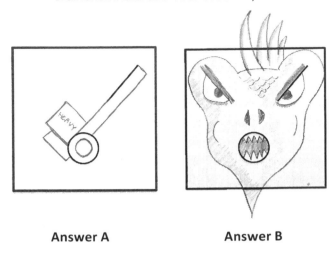

Answer A   **Answer B**

Once again, this is an example of a question that if you answered this many times, you would no doubt come up with improved creative possibilities. Answer A is a simpler answer with little detail added. The circle is also used for something very obvious (a wheel). Answer B displays more detail and goes outside the box. It appears to be more original than Answer A and is therefore more creative. Nevertheless, faces are one of the things that human brains naturally look for and recognize in shapes. As a result, this type of drawing (if not the exact face) might still be fairly obvious to many people. Very creative answers to these types of questions sometimes incorporate the original lines in such a way that they are not at all obvious in the final picture.

6. If money grew on trees, what would you do?

This is an imagination type exercise (see Chapter 9) and a lot of fun can be had answering questions like this:

- Quit my job and become a gardener.

- Look forward to the fall.

- We would all be talking about "leaves" instead of "money."

- Every time your kids asked for money you could send them outside.

- Pay the bills with apples.

- Stop cutting down trees. Deforestation would become too expensive!

7. What do you see in the picture below?

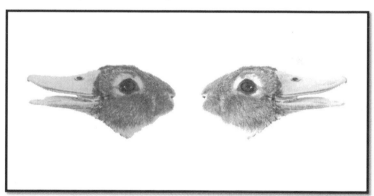

This picture is one of my Brainarium logos based on a well-known illusion. If you look closely you can see:

- Two ducks facing away from each other.

- Two rabbits facing each other.

- A duck and a rabbit facing the same direction.

Moving away from the literal, you can start to create other ideas:

- Angry ducks.

- Rabbits kissing.

- A funky bowtie.

- A mask.

- Presidential candidates!

If you have read these answers in this appendix immediately after reading Chapter 4, I strongly suggest that you look at them again when you have read the rest of the book as the techniques and ideas should make more sense then.

Appendix 2

Key Quotes

By the author ...

- About the only thing you do which requires no creativity is breathing!

- The only sensible approach to creativity (and to life) is a whole-brained one.

- If you use it, your brain continues to develop throughout your life.

- We actually have a choice about how healthy we want our brains to be.

- You have at least a $100 million piece of equipment sitting in your head!

- Because creativity inherently involves something new, it is ideal for training your brain.

- Creativity is enjoyable and can relieve stress for anyone, regardless of how healthy they otherwise are.

- Creativity is a fundamental purpose of being human.

- Who wants to be an ant?!

- Welcome to the Creative Age!

- When a five-year-old enters Kindergarten today, we have no idea exactly what world they will find when they finish their education.

- To thrive in our future world, you will have to be a lifelong learner.

- There are certain precautions you should take to avoid the risk of hurting your mental or creative attitude.

- The power of thoughtful, sincere encouragement is amazing.

- Your creative diet is important for your creative health.

- Remember every rule can be broken except this one.

- People are more observant and creative when faced with a fresh stimulus.

- Creative Strength exercises help generate ideas.

- Creative Stamina exercises help evaluate whether the ideas are original and have value.

- The bigger the ambition, the greater the chance of creativity.

- Collaboration is one of the best ways to be creative.

- You can connect anything to anything.

- Almost no adults get recess time when they are at work!

- Children do their thinking *inside* the box.

- The process of being creative is likely to open you up to possibilities that you were not aware of.

- When you use your imagination, there is often a way of making things work.

The two most important words in the English language are "what if?"

(Let's not forget these either):

"Creativity" is not an elitist word.

Everyone is creative.

Creativity is essential to a healthy, happy, purposeful life.

Creativity is essential for future human success.

Creativity can be learned and should be exercised.

Creativity should be encouraged and appreciated whenever possible.

By others ...

"We've got to do something about the mental lifespan, to extend it out and into the body's lifespan." – Michael Merzenich

"Neurons that fire together wire together." – Carla Shatz

"Artists become creative experts by practicing how to be creative." – Charles Limb

"Creative expression is our ultimate demonstration of who we are in life." – Brendon Burchard

"The most promising way to happiness is, perhaps, through creativity, through literally creating a fulfilling life for yourself by identifying some unique talent or passion and devoting a good part of your energy to it, forever." – Kalle Lasn and Bruce Grierson

"To get the full value of joy, you must have somebody to divide it with." – Mark Twain

"Creativity is an original idea that has value." – Sir Ken Robinson

"We are putting creativity into the category of entertainment instead of education. And that's a mistake." – Charles Limb

"Creativity is as important in education as literacy." – Sir Ken Robinson

"Educational systems that catalyze imagination and creativity will be the winners." – Howard Gardner

"A few years ago, [companies] could see the competition coming. Today, the competition's often invisible until it's too late." – IBM Global C-Suite Report

"Most companies are built for continuous improvement, not discontinuous innovation." – Gary Hamel

"Children enter school as question marks and come out as periods." – Neil Postman

"We don't stop playing because we grow old. We grow old because we stop playing." – Unknown

"Every child is an artist. The problem is how to remain an artist when you grow up." – Pablo Picasso

"Almost all creativity involves purposeful play." – Abraham Maslow

"Imagination is more important than knowledge." – Albert Einstein

- "New product ideas that anticipate the future are 10 times more predictive of success than those that simply listen to the voice of the customer." – Doug Hall

- "You get ideas from daydreaming. You get ideas from being bored. You get ideas all the time." – Neil Gaiman

- "That sounds interesting. How can we make it work?" – Paul Sloane

Appendix 3

Creative Equipment

Luckily, creative equipment is not as expensive as gym equipment. Aside from your $100 million brain, most other equipment costs only a few dollars.

Basics

You will want a way to record your ideas. A pencil and paper are sufficient for this. You might want a notebook to record all your ideas in one place. Smartphones and computers are also fantastic ways of recording information both in written and audio form. Choose what works best for you.

When being creative, I still prefer working on paper as it is easier for me to see all my ideas at once, compared to the limited display of a computer.

For inspiration

Much inspiration is obtained from new experiences (such as meeting new people, going to new places or doing new activities). Nevertheless, you can have certain items at home or work that will give you inspiration when you are not able to have a new experience. Such creative equipment might include:

- Children's stories (I especially like picture books. If I could choose, I'd make all adult books have pictures too!).

- Photos and pictures.

- Magazines and books.

- The internet – just about anything and everything is on there!

- Toys and games.

- Objects, ornaments, and souvenirs – they might bring back memories of experiences or they might prompt your imagination.

A creative toolkit for your desk

Children get to play with toys all the time. Such play is healthy and stimulates their amazing creativity – their toys are creative tools. Why shouldn't adults have their own set of creative tools to play with on their desk to help stimulate creativity?

Anyone can gather a creative toolkit together from easily accessible supplies. Below are some suggestions. You don't need all of these and you could also add any other objects you wish.

- A pencil

- Some paper

- A few colored markers/crayons

- A ball of *Blu-Tack* (or similar putty)

- A few *Post-it Notes*

- Some paper clips

- A piece of string

- Some elastic bands

- A pair of scissors

- A glass of water

- Some stones/pebbles

- A small tray/lid of sand

What can you do with these? There are some suggested exercises below. By now I would hope that you realize that you can do these as suggested, adapt these as you wish or come up with your own creative ideas. That is the very essence of creativity.

- **Play**
  Simply do anything you feel like doing with any of the objects! What comes into your mind? Do you use any of them together?

- **Waterworld**
  What do things look like when submerged in water? How does the perspective change? What happens to the objects (or drawings you make) when they get wet?

- **Raft challenge**
  What can you make float in the water? Can you use other items to make heavy things (e.g. pebbles) float?

- **Sculpture**
  What can you make out of the materials? You could challenge yourself to use just one object/material or to use a certain number of them.

- **Engineering challenges**
  What's the tallest structure you can build? What's the strongest structure you can build (i.e. to carry the heaviest load)? Can you make a bridge over a river?

- **Machine**
  Can you make a machine? Can you make it move or have moving parts?

- *Post-it* **Art**
  What can you draw on a *Post-it Note*? A doodle or a masterpiece? Modern, Abstract, Classical? 2D or 3D? Can you make enough exhibits to hold an exhibition?

- **Office Olympics**
  Design your own Office Olympic events with the items. Think about how to make competitive events involving speed, distance, height, accuracy, endurance etc. This can be a fun activity with a number of people.

- **Pimp My Glass of Water**
  Use the items to jazz up your glass of water and be the envy of your office!

- **Zen Garden**
  Zen gardens are used in the Far East as a source of meditation and relaxation. Put some of the pebbles in the tray. Use the pencil to rake the sand in lines/circles or any design you wish.

- **What else?**
  What other ideas do you have?

Appendix 4

About The Author & Brainarium Exercises

Following careers in law and teaching, Stuart is a now a motivational speaker, consultant, and coach who is determined to get everyone in the world to exercise their creativity. He came 3rd in the Toastmasters World Championship of Public Speaking. He and one of his 2nd Grade classes in England had a piece of art exhibited in the National Gallery in London.

For more information about having Stuart speak at your next event or to get free creative updates and tips please go to www.brainarium.com or connect with him on social media. Every day he publishes creative exercises to help train the brain. Some samples are on the next pages. Feel free to check them out and share your creativity with the Brainarium community.

Email: stuart@brainarium.com

Instagram: @stuartjpink

Twitter: @PinkStuart

Facebook: facebook.com/brainarium/

Creative Exercise #3

Combine 2 different animals to create a new, hybrid animal.

E.g. OCTOCOW (drawing optional!)

Creative Exercise #17

What is the worst ice cream flavor you can imagine?

Brainarium

Creative Exercise #30

What story is being told here?

Brainarium

Creative Exercise #38

If your life had a soundtrack ...

... what song would play when you leave the house?   Brainarium

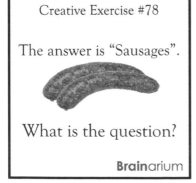

Creative Exercise #78

The answer is "Sausages".

What is the question?

Brainarium

Creative Exercise #84

The main reason we should have winter all year round is ...

Brainarium

188

Creative Exercise #91

What would be the strangest thing if life were upside down?

Brainarium

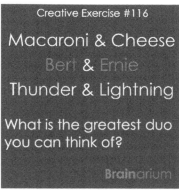

Creative Exercise #116

Macaroni & Cheese
Bert & Ernie
Thunder & Lightning

What is the greatest duo you can think of?

Brainarium

Creative Exercise #126

If vegetables described personalities, which vegetable would you be? Why?!

Brainarium

Creative Exercise #161

Describe your life so far in 10 words.

Brainarium

Creative Exercise #181

How will language change in the future?

Brainarium

Creative Exercise #234

What is it?

Brainarium

Appendix 5

References

Chapter 1

[1] http://blogs.harvard.edu/abinazir/2011/06/15/what-are-chances-you-would-be-born/

[2] It is commonly estimated that there are 10^{80} atoms in the universe. https://en.wikipedia.org/wiki/Observable_universe

[3] http://www.cnn.com/2009/HEALTH/10/12/woman.brain.index.html?iref=24hours

[4] http://www.livescience.com/7822-girl-sees-fine-brain.html

[5] http://www.onthebrain.com/brain-plasticity/

[6] N. Doidge, 2007, The Brain That Changes Itself: Stories of Personal Triumph from the Frontiers of Brain Science. New York: Penguin Books, 242.

[7] http://www.whitehouse.gov/share/brain-initiative

[8] http://www.phy.duke.edu/~hsg/363/table-images/brain-vs-computer.html

[9] http://blogs.scientificamerican.com/news-blog/computers-have-a-lot-to-learn-from-2009-03-10/

[10] http://www.top500.org

[11] http://www.nextplatform.com/2016/06/20/look-inside-chinas-chart-topping-new-supercomputer/

Chapter 2

[12] http://www.statista.com/statistics/236123/us-fitness-center--health-club-memberships/
https://www.franchisehelp.com/industry-reports/fitness-industry-report/

[13] AARP 2015 Survey on Brain Health.

[14] N. Doidge, 2007, The Brain That Changes Itself: Stories of Personal Triumph from the Frontiers of Brain Science. New York: Penguin Books, 85.

[15] Ibid., 43.

[16] https://en.wikipedia.org/wiki/Carla_J._Shatz

[17] C. Limb, M.D. interviewed in 2015, The Brain: The Ultimate Guide. New York: Ben Harris, 73.

[18] N. Doidge, 2007, The Brain That Changes Itself: Stories of Personal Triumph from the Frontiers of Brain Science. New York: Penguin Books, 78.

[19] Ibid., 59.

[20] Ibid., 201-202.

[21] E. Shackell, L. Standing, (2007). Mind Over Matter: Mental Training Increases Physical Strength. *North American Journal of Psychology* 9(1), pp. 189-200.

[22] For example see http://www.lumosity.com/, http://www.neuronation.com/, http://www.brainhq.com, http://www.brainmetrix.com, https://stayingsharp.aarp.org/games.

[23] http://longevity3.stanford.edu/blog/2014/10/15/the-consensus-on-the-brain-training-industry-from-the-scientific-community-2/

[24] http://www.alz.org/facts/overview.asp

[25] Banking Against Alzheimer's, D. Bennett, Scientific American, July/August 2016, 29-37.

[26] http://www.moma.org/meetme/

[27] http://www.moma.org/momaorg/shared/pdfs/docs/meetme/MeetMe_FULL.pdf., 60, 65.

[28] http://www.nccata.org/#!research/cihc

[29] M. Csikszentmihalyi, 1990, Flow. New York: HarperCollins.

[30] V. Frankl, 1959, 1962, 1984, Man's Search for Meaning: An Introduction to Logotherapy. New York: Simon & Schuster, Inc., 84.

[31] K. Lasn and B. Grierson (2000), Why is America so Depressed? http://www.utne.com/mind-and-body/america-the-blue.aspx?PageId=6

Chapter 3

[32] K. Robinson, 2001, 2011, Out of Our Minds: Learning to be Creative, Chichester: Capstone, 151.

[33] http://www.myownpetballoon.com

[34] D. Pink, 2008, A Whole New Mind, London: Marshall Cavendish, 48-57.

[35] http://www.oxfordmartin.ox.ac.uk/downloads/academic/The_Future_of_Employment.pdf

[36] http://www.bls.gov/news.release/pdf/nlsyth.pdf

37 H. Bakhshi, C.B. Frey, and M. Osborne, (2015) Creativity vs. Robots: The Creative Economy and the Future of Employment, Nesta. http://www.nesta.org.uk/sites/default/files/creativity_vs._robots_wv.pdf

38 http://www.telegraph.co.uk/news/science/science-news/8316534/Welcome-to-the-information-age-174-newspapers-a-day.html

39 http://www3.weforum.org/docs/WEF_ASEAN_HumanCapitalOutlook.pdf

40 C. Limb, M.D. interviewed in 2015, The Brain: The Ultimate Guide. New York: Ben Harris, 73.

41 https://www.ted.com/talks/ken_robinson_says_schools_kill_creativity?language=en

42 H. Gardner interviewed in Brain World, Spring 2015, 46.

43 http://www.p21.org/our-work/4cs-research-series

44 Ananiadou, K. and M. Claro (2009), "21st Century Skills and Competences for New Millennium Learners in OECD Countries", OECD Education Working Papers, No. 41, OECD Publishing. http://www.oecd.org/officialdocuments/publicdisplaydocumentpdf/?cote=EDU/WKP(2009)20&doclanguage=en

45 Judy Lemke, CIO of Schneider interviewed in 2015, Redefining Boundaries: Insights from the Global C-suite Study, IBM, 1.

46 2015, Redefining Boundaries: Insights from the Global C-suite Study, IBM, 24.

47 Ibid., 3.

48 P. Sloan, 2003, 2006, The Leader's Guide to Lateral Thinking Skills: Unlocking the creativity and innovation in you and your team., London: Kogan Page, 5.

49 2010, Capitalizing on Complexity: Insights from the Global Chief Executive Officer Study, IBM, 24.

50 http://www.skillsfuture.sg/credit http://www.economist.com/news/special-report/21714169-technological-change-demands-stronger-and-more-continuous-connections-between-education

51 H. Bakhshi, C.B. Frey, and M. Osborne, (2015) Creativity vs. Robots: The Creative Economy and the Future of Employment, Nesta. http://www.nesta.org.uk/sites/default/files/creativity_vs._robots_wv.pdf

52 http://www.worldhunger.org/2015-world-hunger-and-poverty-facts-and-statistics/#hunger-number

53 http://water.org/water-crisis/water-sanitation-facts/

54 http://www.hipporoller.org

Chapter 4

55 R. Von Oech, 1983, 1990, 1998, A Whack On The Side Of The Head. New York: Barnes & Noble Books, 169.

Chapter 5

[56] http://www.fastcompany.com/59549/failure-doesnt-suck

[57] http://www.youtube.com/watch?v=Ylmfo7t8Wec

[58] http://thereallyterribleorchestra.com/wordpress/

[59] For example see http://thesecondprinciple.com/creativity/children-creativity/killingcreativityinchildren/

[60] http://www.businessinsider.com/google-20-percent-time-policy-2015-4

Chapter 6

[61] http://www.businessinsider.com/jim-rohn-youre-the-average-of-the-five-people-you-spend-the-most-time-with-2012-7

[62] http://www1.hansgrohe.com/assets/at--de/1404_Hansgrohe_Select_ConsumerSurvey_EN.pdf

Chapter 7

[63] http://www.kindsnacks.com/about/#slide-two

[64] E. de Bono, 1985, 2000, Six Thinking Hats. London: Penguin Books.

[65] http://www.minyanville.com/sectors/consumer/articles/Tesla-Motors-Inc2527s-Elon-Musk-hyperloop/7/16/2013/id/50827

[66] http://www.pocket-lint.com/news/132405-what-is-elon-musk-s-700mph-hyperloop-the-subsonic-train-explained

[67] http://www.timeanddate.com/date/birthday.html

Chapter 8

[68] It took Søren Eilers from the University of Copenhagen nearly 21 days to calculate the actual figure of 915,103,765!
http://time.com/3977789/lego-brickumentary-math-professor-combinations/
http://www.math.ku.dk/~eilers/lego.html

[69] http://www.gamezebo.com/2009/05/22/interview-plants-vs-zombies-creator-george-fan/

[70] http://www.nationaldaycalendar.com/national-open-an-umbrella-indoors-day-march-13/

[71] http://creativethinking.net/leonardo-davincis-ideabox/#sthash.0rjD9Gxy.dpbs
Michalko also describes the Idea Box in his great book Thinkertoys: M. Michalko, 2006, 1991, Thinkertoys. New York: Ten Speed Press, 117-125.

Chapter 9

72 R. Von Oech, 1983, 1990, 1998, A Whack On The Side Of The Head. New York: Barnes & Noble Books, 27.

73 http://www.forbes.com/sites/leeigel/2015/01/15/the-common-core-is-taking-away-kids-recess-and-that-makes-no-sense/#f7aac5153d10

74 Some of the people this quote is attributed to are Benjamin Franklin, Oliver Wendell Holmes, George Bernard Shaw and G. Stanley Hall - https://en.wikiquote.org/wiki/Growing_old

75 http://www.parentingscience.com/benefits-of-play.html

76 P. Reynolds, 2003, The Dot. Somerville, MA: Candlewick Press.

77 http://fredmandell.com

78 M. Michalko, 2006, 1991, Thinkertoys. New York: Ten Speed Press, 261-7.

79 For doodles of US Presidents, see: http://mentalfloss.com/article/54412/21-presidential-doodles

80 S. Brown, 2014, The Doodle Revolution: New York: Portfolio/Penguin.

81 http://www.toastmasters.org - an organization to practice public speaking.

82 http://www.tomwujec.com/design-projects/marshmallow-challenge/

83 http://www.toyhalloffame.org/toys/cardboard-box

84 http://www.youtube.com/watch?v=faIFNkdq96U and http://cainesarcade.com

85 http://imagination.is/our-projects/cardboard-challenge/

86 http://quoteinvestigator.com/2013/01/01/einstein-imagination/

87 http://www.nytimes.com/2015/11/01/opinion/sunday/the-light-beam-rider.html?_r=0

88 D. Hall, 1995, 2008, JUMP START Your Brain v2.0. Cincinnati: Clerisy Press, 238.

89 Darya L. Zabelina and Michael D. Robinson, 2010, Child's Play: Facilitating the Originality of Creative Output by a Priming Manipulation. See http://www.psychologytoday.com/files/attachments/34246/zabelina-robinson-2010a.pdf.

90 http://www.inc.com/chris-winfield/is-boredom-the-ultimate-creativity-hack.html

91 P. Howard, 2006, The Owner's Manual for The Brain, 3rd Ed., Austin: Bard Press, 190-2.

Chapter 10

92 P. Sloan, 2003, 2006, The Leader's Guide to Lateral Thinking Skills: Unlocking the creativity and innovation in you and your team., London: Kogan Page, 124.

93 See The Great Courses: The Creative Thinker's Toolkit, lecture 6.

Made in the USA
San Bernardino, CA
01 August 2018